"Dale Ledbetter and Connie Becker have penned a new book that is a "must read" for anyone who has any interest in investing in the stock market and wants to understand why innocent people get swindled out of their hard earned money. It clears the fog of deceits perpetrated by Wall Street manipulators."

Michael Levy,
Author of *Cutting Truths* and
Invest With a Genius.

"This comprehensive book exposes many Wall Street secrets and shows investors how to protect themselves and make sound investment decisions. It should be required reading for every investor."

Rick Woolf,
Former IRS Criminal Investigations Special
Agent and Registered Investment Advisor
for over 30 years.

"This book hits hard, tells it like it is and offers effective ways to fight back."

Andrew Stoltmann,
Attorney, Investor Advocate and Adjunct
Professor of Securities Law at
Northwestern University School of Law.

"The lessons of this book are vital for all investors regardless of their level of experience. The authors don't mince words. They tell it like it is!"

John Primeau,
Community Banker for over 40 years.

"Buyer beware" has always been the central theme of Wall Street and many have written on this subject. Yet, Dale and Connie have done a spectacular job of both summarizing the basics of fraud in the market as well as providing the reader an up to date view of the latest tricks of the trade.

**William S. Shepherd, JD, LLM
(Securities Regulation)**
Worked over 20 years for Wall Street.
Founder of one of the nation's largest law
firms representing investors.

How
Wall Street
Rips You Off

-and what you can do to defend yourself

Written By:
Dale Ledbetter
and
Connie Becker

LEI Publishing

Published by LEI Publishing

LEI publishes in a variety of print and electronic formats and by print-on-demand.

Book cover design by Michelle McElhannon, 2012

Library of Congress Cataloging-in-Publication Data:
Library of Congress Control Number: 2012913645

Printed in the United States of America

ISBN 978-0-9678769-1-7

This book is dedicated to the countless clients we've had the privilege of working with whose sad stories have touched our hearts.

✱✱✱

"We should learn to benefit from the mistakes of others because our own make us poorer."
Anonymous

Acknowledgments

This book would not have been possible without the help and support of many people.

First, the authors want to thank the many clients we have been privileged to work with and represent in the past. Many of their stories are shared in this book. In order to protect their privacy they must remain nameless, but you all know who you are and we offer our most sincere gratitude.

Special thanks to Bob DeLoach, law partner at Ledbetter & Associates, who has contributed wonderful ideas, exceptional editing and has stepped in to carry an additional workload while the authors devoted time and energy to the completion of this book. Similar expressions go to others who have been associated with our firm during the time the book was being prepared: Bill Gladden, Jim Graven, Adam Nativ, Dan Woska, Steve Oggel, Jim Hall and Tomas Jodar.

Our legal mentors, Jan Atlas and George Fleming, also deserve our gratitude.

The Public Investors Bar Association (PIABA) has been an endless fountain of support and information. There are so many PIABA members to thank. Let us begin by apologizing to the many who are not mentioned. However, special thanks for knowledge shared and lessons learned go out to Seth Lippner, Jeff Sonn, Bill Shepherd, Jeff Erez, Andrew Stoltmann, Dave Neuman, Kirk Reasonover, Scott Beall, Chuck Austin, Kristian Kraszewski, Andy Campbell, Peter Mougey, and Richard Frankowski. Again, thanks go to others whose names are not included, but whose contributions will never be forgotten.

We received ongoing help from experts we have worked with over the years including Craig McCann, Eddie O'Neal, Jim Gatewood, Jim French and Joyce Wagner.

A special thank you goes out to Dan Woska for his contribution of time, ideas and experiences.

The work could never have been completed without the tireless typing, editing and suggested improvements made by Azaly Colome and Michelle McElhannon.

We would also be remiss if we didn't thank our many friends within the securities industry who shared their knowledge and experience. Again, their contributions must remain anonymous to protect their privacy and, in some cases, to protect their jobs.

About the Authors

Dale Ledbetter

"...we shall fight on the beaches, we shall fight on the landing grounds, we shall fight in the fields and in the streets, we shall fight in the hills; we shall never surrender."

Winston Churchill's famous quote effectively summarizes Dale Ledbetter's ambition to give Main Street a fighting chance against Wall Street.

As founder of Ledbetter & Associates, PA, Dale Ledbetter is a national leader in the battle against the injustice that investors endure when interacting with brokerage firms. He represents investors from all over the United States and worldwide in FINRA arbitrations to recover losses caused by the negligence and corruption of Wall Street. The firm represents not just individual claimants, but banks, insurance companies, thrifts, and pension funds.

Securities litigation requires not just legal knowledge, background and experience, but a thorough mastery of the products and how the products can be abused. With his more than 40 years of diverse experience in the securities industry, he is now capturing attention nationwide as a leading investor advocate.

Dale is a graduate of Rhodes College in Memphis, Tennessee and received his law degree from George Washington University Law Center. He is a member of the Bar in Florida, Tennessee and the District of Columbia. Dale served as a staff member to three U.S. Senators and a Vice-President. He was also appointed as a delegate to the White House Conference on Small Business and served as counsel for the International Council of Shopping Centers. He is a long-time member of the Public Investors Arbitration Bar Association, the largest organization of lawyers who represent investors in arbitration claims against broker dealers.

Dale is a member of the board of directors for the American Association of Collegiate Student Athletes (AACSA, Inc.), a non-profit organization established to increase the graduation rates of collegiate student athletes. He belongs to the National Speakers Association and is a frequent speaker on investment related topics. He has entertained audiences as an accomplished magician and is a longstanding member of the world-famous Magic Castle in Hollywood, California. He also serves on the Board of Directors of the Hypoglycemia Support Foundation.

Connie Becker

Connie Becker has a Masters Degree in Business Administration and has worked as a paralegal for almost 20 years, mostly in securities litigation. Connie is a team member at Ledbetter & Associates, PA and has played a key role in hundreds of securities arbitration cases. The cases Connie has worked on have involved claims dating back from the 2000 dot com crash to the more recent credit crisis. She has extensive experience on cases involving stock options, commodities, mutual funds, ETFs, structured finance and variable rate annuities. Her daily efforts have been focused on helping investors to understand and navigate through the securities arbitration process.

Connie earned a Bachelor of Arts in German Studies from Western Washington University, a Paralegal Certificate from Highline College in Seattle, Washington, and a Masters Degree in Business Administration from Nova Southeastern University in Fort Lauderdale, Florida. She is an associate member of ACFE, the Association of Certified Fraud Examiners. Connie also serves as an arbitrator and actively recruits new arbitrators for securities arbitration. A native of the Pacific Northwest, she currently enjoys the sunshine of South Florida where she lives with her husband and children.

Table of Contents

Introduction

There are hundreds of books describing past financial crises and predicting yet more crises in the future. There are countless books advising investors on how to invest their money. The get rich quick schemes often sell like hotcakes both at bookstores and at the aggressive sales seminars put on by many authors. There are many books written about specific areas within the investment universe such as mutual funds, annuities, stocks and bonds.

This book is designed to be different. It is hoped that it can serve as a "one-stop source" for many different groups and individuals. It should be noted that when the term Wall Street is used in this book it is used to refer to broker dealers who are registered with the Financial Industry Regulatory Authority (FINRA), a Self-Regulatory Organization (SRO), whether the firm be located within the New York City financial center or in any other area throughout the United States.

The various sections of this book will walk readers through obstacles faced by the average investor in dealing with Wall Street. The first objective of this book is to explore the many ways in which Wall Street rips off investors. The second is to debunk the myth that FINRA provides meaningful protection for investors against Wall Street negligence and abuse. The third major objective is to provide specific steps investors can take to defend themselves against the aggressive onslaught of Wall Street profiteers. Ultimately, the goal is to provide readers with the knowledge, tools and strategies that can be employed as defenses against becoming a Wall Street victim. Sadly, readers will learn that the system is designed to reward dishonesty and the lack of transparency.

Special attention is paid to three areas which have been sources of particularly egregious conduct on the part of Wall Street in recent years. Mutual funds, annuities (particularly equity indexed annuities and variable rate annuities), and structured finance products are used to victimize millions of trusting investors around the world. It is particularly important that readers have an

[1]

understanding of how these products are being successfully utilized by Wall Street to victimize investors.

Wall Street doesn't solely do business with individual investors. Pension funds and other institutional investors have also been victims. A chapter within this book details ways in which Wall Street has victimized pension funds.

The Appendix offers additional sources of information that can be helpful to investors seeking to better understand the securities industry.

There are a series of horror stories presented throughout the book. The names of the wrongdoers, as well as the victims, have been changed or omitted from these stories. Some stories are strategically placed near the specific area to which they relate. Others are placed at random. Some are consolidations of experiences suffered by multiple investors, but all are based on fact.

This book is **NOT** written to encourage unjustified complaints. We do not believe in bringing frivolous actions against broker dealers. To do so has a negative impact on the many valid claims that exist and that should be brought by victims of fraud or negligence. There are honest brokers that understand their duties and are dedicated to the best interests of their clients. Sometimes, their efforts on behalf of clients are made in spite of management's encouragement to do otherwise. Only the guilty should be pursued.

In order to recover securities losses, an investor can't simply say, "I lost money." There are risks; and the brokerage industry, as participants loudly proclaim, does not "insure" against losses. We hear from potential clients on a regular basis who believe, that simply because they lost money, the broker dealer is liable. That is blatantly false.

For investors to recover, they must show a link between what the broker dealer did and the losses that occurred. These "causal" connections must be made and it is irresponsible to bring an action when no such link exists. This book will help investors evaluate factual situations and help them establish causal connections between their losses and the acts of their broker dealer.

This book should not be read like a novel starting on page one and going through to the end. Look at the table of contents, or look through the pages, and find the areas of greatest interest to you. Each section of the book stands on its own and provides both warnings about misdeeds and directions to avoid becoming a victim.

In our practice we have seen thousands of abused victims. This book is not an attempt to sell a product or any investment idea or concept. It is offered as a shield for often defenseless investors. It is hoped that this book will help countless investors to avoid being added to Wall Street's list of innocent victims. If only a few avoid the pitfalls and pain which have been inflicted on so many, then the work that went into producing this book will have been worthwhile.

It is hoped that this book will help many readers from ever needing to seek services from our office or from any other group of attorneys representing abused investors. However, do not be misled. The way the system is set up makes it virtually impossible for investors to avoid some level of abuse if they choose to have an account with a registered broker dealer. Because the financial markets involve access to the money of others, some participants succumb to the temptations to abuse the trust given to them. Given management demands on brokers, commission compensation structures, and emphasis on production rather than client success, the protection of investors is all too often left as an afterthought. Thus, it is important to select financial professionals carefully and hold them accountable if they engage in misconduct.

Lastly, but certainly not of least importance, it is hoped that the book will provide both entertainment and education for those who want to know more about money, investments and the tremendous impact they both have on the daily lives of most every human being.

[3]

***

HORROR STORY

The theme of this book is that it is easier to avoid losing your money than it is to try to get it back. Former NBA star Horace Grant learned this the hard way.

In 2008, attorney Andrew Stoltmann filed a claim on Grant's behalf against a brokerage firm. A California arbitration panel heard the case in August 2009 and awarded Grant $1,450,000.

In his Claim, Grant alleged that the broker dealer engaged in a reckless plan of selling highly speculative funds and substantially misrepresented and omitted material information regarding the risks of owning the funds.

Following the award, the broker dealer filed a Motion to Vacate the arbitration award in federal court in California.

Investors have been led to believe that FINRA arbitration is final and binding. That is hardly the case. The broker dealer's defenses denying Grant's allegations were rejected by the arbitration panel. In its Motion to Vacate the broker dealer asked the court to order a re-hearing before a new panel of arbitrators on the grounds that the arbitrators were partial and biased against the broker dealer, were guilty of misbehavior and exceeded their powers by issuing an irrational award in manifest disregard of the law.

In denying the Motion to Vacate, the District Court set out the limited grounds for vacating an arbitration award:

> "...review of an arbitration award is both limited and highly deferential, and the arbitration award may be vacated only if it is completely irrational or constitutes a manifest disregard of the law." Comedy Club, Inc. v. Improv W. Assoc., 553F3d 1227, 1288 (9th Cir. 2009).

The Court noted further, "Arbitrators need provide only a fundamentally fair hearing," and then added:

"A hearing is fundamentally fair if it meets the minimal requirements of fairness, adequate notice, a hearing on the evidence and an impartial decision by the arbitrator." <u>Sunshine Min. Cov. United Steelworkers of Am.</u>, AFL-CIO, CLD, 823 F2d 1295 (9th Cir. 1987).

After a 26 page discussion the court concluded:

"...Petitioner has the burden of showing partiality or bias, and any doubts or uncertainties must be resolved in favor of upholding the Arbitration Award...because it is speculative that the arbitrators' statements made during the above-mentioned break represent anything more than informal banter, and Petitioner was nonetheless, given a full and fair opportunity to present its case, Petitioner has not shown that it was deprived of a fundamentally fair hearing. Finally, because the Arbitration Award represents a figure that was discussed by the parties several times, and is consistent with California law, the Arbitration Award is neither completely irrational, nor in manifest disregard of the law. Accordingly, the court declines to vacate the Arbitration Award."

That Order was entered on June 30, 2010, almost two years from the time of the initial arbitration. However, it did not end there and Grant was not paid the award. On July 10, 2010 the broker dealer filed a Notice of Appeal with the 9th Circuit Court of Appeals in California. The appeal, as of this writing, is still pending with a decision not likely before sometime in 2013. Grant, who originally filed his case in March 2008, will have waited almost 5 years for a final result. It is unlikely that the U.S. Supreme Court would hear this case but there is no assurance that a further appeal could not be filed.

In the meantime, Grant awaits payment.
***

Section 1

Examining Wall Street Rip Offs

***

HORROR STORY

"Here sir, just sign on this line and we will do the rest." If any investor hears this, or a similar instruction, they should be forewarned that trouble is just around the corner.

An elderly retiree asked her nephew, who held Power of Attorney over her brokerage account, to execute a change in beneficiary on an annuity contract sold to her by her broker. The nephew contacted the brokerage firm and was sent a change of beneficiary form. He asked the broker for instructions on how to fill out the form and where to sign. The broker told him where to sign, uttering the infamous sentence, "Here sir, just sign on this line and we will do the rest." The retiree's nephew did as instructed and sent back the form. The broker assured him that he had spoken with the insurance company and that he knew "how to handle these things."

Shortly after the signed form was sent in, the retiree passed away. Just prior to her death, the nephew received a letter from the insurance company notifying him that the beneficiary change form he had signed was incomplete. He signed the new form, making the requested changes and returned the form directly to the insurance company. The broker assured the nephew that "it happens all the time" and it "was no big deal."

The new beneficiary made a claim for proceeds under the policy. The insurance company said, due to the negligence and confusion, they would not honor the request without a notarized waiver from the prior beneficiary. Sadly, the prior beneficiary refused to cooperate. The successor beneficiary sought help from the brokerage firm whose negligence had created the problem. The broker dealer disavowed any responsibility.

The proper beneficiary had to hire an attorney to help sort out the matter. By the time a resolution was reached with the insurance company, the brokerage firm and the prior beneficiary, proceeds to the successor beneficiary were reduced by over 50%.

***

Chapter 1
How Wall Street Rips Off Investors

Having Investors Sign Inaccurate Account Opening Documents

This may well be the most important chapter of this book. Errors or omissions in the account opening documentation can give a brokerage firm *carte blanche* to run amok in an investor's account. If a problem develops in an account, the same shortcomings can doom any hopes an investor might have to get justice. Be careful in opening a new account. Use this book as an excuse to go to your brokerage firm and conduct a thorough review of all existing documents. Sadly, there are often great differences between what an investor is told verbally and what is reflected in the written account opening documents.

The most important lesson you may learn from this book is that the process of being ripped off by Wall Street does not begin with the first transaction. It begins much earlier. It begins when the account is first opened. The account opening documents create a written contractual agreement between the investor and the brokerage firm. Investors should be aware that these documents are carefully drafted by the brokerage firm's lawyers for the firm's protection, not the investor's. Account opening documents are always treated very casually by investors. The forms are often completed at the beginning of the relationship with the firm, during the "honeymoon phase" of the relationship.

The broker is, above all, a salesperson and is generally not placing the investor's protection as the first priority. The last thing the broker wants to do is talk about risks, risk exposure or the downside of the investment experience. He wants to paint a rosy picture of positive results, great success and a worry-free future.

It is essential for an investor who opens a brokerage account to have a solid understanding of the information required on the customer application and the purpose for which the firm is requesting that information. It is true that the information may be used to help the financial advisor assist the customer with investment objectives and financial goals. However, the information supplied on the application may be, and often is, used to protect the broker dealer and is often used against the interest of the customer if a problem arises. As simple as it sounds, an investor needs to make sure the information provided in the account opening documents is complete and accurate. Otherwise, in a dispute, the firm will accuse the customer of providing incomplete information. Never forget that the brokerage firm is selling products and has far different objectives than you do.

The information set out below will serve as a helpful guide to interpreting and understanding how best to complete the mandatory forms when opening a new brokerage account.

A. Account Type:

Generally, the first piece of information requested is account-type. There are several types of brokerage accounts, each with varying levels of service provided by the brokerage firm. Examples of the most common types of accounts for retail investors include:

- **Cash**: This type of account allows only for cash purchases of securities. No purchases on margin are permitted.

- **Margin**: This is an account in which the investor may borrow funds to purchase securities using existing holdings as collateral.

It is important to know that some brokerage firms do not clearly distinguish a margin account as a separate account type. Many general account opening documents include a margin loan agreement clause within another type of account agreement. If a customer does not want to use margin, it is recommended to specifically instruct the broker against using margin to make any purchases in the account and make sure the documents reflect that arrangement.

[10]

There are many risks for the investor when it comes to investing on margin. To protect themselves, customers need to be fully aware of what type of account they are opening. A public customer should be extremely wary and should never agree to highly risky margin transactions.

As an investor, ask yourself a simple question. Would you go to the bank, borrow money and use those funds to trade securities? If your answer is no, you want no part of a margin account. That is exactly what you are doing when you enter into transactions using funds borrowed on margin. Beware! Margin equals high risk.

- **Options**: An option is a contract that gives the buyer the right, but not the obligation, to buy or sell an underlying asset at a specific price on, or before, a certain date. An option, just like a stock or bond, is a security. It is also a binding contract with strictly defined terms and properties. This type of account allows the customer to establish options positions separate from, or in addition to, securities positions. There are many different options strategies with varying degrees of risk. It is not wise to sign any forms agreeing to options without a complete understanding of these investment strategies. As with margin, the use of options should almost never be undertaken by retail investors.

Brokerage firms lure investors with stories of grand success. It is also true that every time there is a lottery, someone wins. However, the odds are astronomically tilted in the direction of failure. The same is true for investors who agree to play the options game.

The danger of agreeing to an options account goes beyond the risks involved with actually doing options trades. A brokerage firm defending itself in litigation will use a customer's stated willingness to trade options (even if the customer has simply checked the appropriate box for options trading, but never actually engaged in options trades!) to argue that the customer has a high

[11]

risk tolerance, even if the strategy is being used in a supposedly conservative manner. Options are for experts.

- **Retirement**: This is a brokerage account established within a retirement plan, such as an Individual Retirement Account (IRA), Simplified Employee Pension (SEP), or 401(k). Generally, investors should select more conservative investment objectives in a retirement account and not place irreplaceable funds at risk.

- **Discretionary**: This is an account where the broker has complete discretion over trades in the account. Opening a discretionary account is like giving the brokerage firm a stack of blank checks. A discretionary account can also be a margin account, an option account, a retirement account or a cash account.

Unless the customer specifically provides authority to the representative through the account opening documents, it is not a discretionary account and the customer must approve every transaction in the account.

B. Income and Net Worth:

The brokerage firm has a right to this information because of their requirement to provide suitable investment recommendations. As with all other information, this information must be complete, accurate and up to date. This includes providing information on any other investments outside of the brokerage firm making the request. This information will be used in combination with all other information provided by the investor for the financial advisor to make investment recommendations. Any major changes, such as retirement, unemployment or significant investments made outside of the brokerage firm, should be disclosed to the firm within a reasonable time frame.

Failure to provide complete information can only hurt the investor. If income and/or net worth are overstated, the firm will use that information to classify the investor as more sophisticated and expose the investor to more risk. If they are understated, the firm may say that the investor had a greater net worth than was disclosed and that is why the investor allowed the firm to take risks in the account. In any event, the slightest inaccuracy can be used against the investor by the broker dealer in a dispute. Don't let your ego take over and allow your net worth to be inflated. Also, don't allow your desire for secrecy to cause you to make meaningful understatements regarding your holdings.

C. Investment Objectives/Risk Tolerance:

All account applications will have a section that requests information about the customer's investment objectives. Most firms request that the customer supply both risk tolerance and investment objective information. In a portfolio with multiple accounts, it is not uncommon for the accounts to have different objectives and risk tolerances. It is in the investor's best interest to be very specific and provide as much detail about the investment objectives and risk tolerance as possible. The broker is required to follow the customer's stated investment objectives so that the recommendations to the investor are appropriate in light of any stated circumstances and risk or return requirements. [1]

Risk tolerance is different from investment objectives. Investment objectives relate to the goal of the account; risk tolerance relates directly to the investor. It describes an investor's ability and willingness to bear the possibility of investments losing value in exchange for the possibility of higher returns. Risk tolerance ranges from conservative to very aggressive. A simple way of looking at risk tolerance involves identifying how much general risk one likes to take financially. Below is an example of a risk tolerance scale.

---

[1] See FINRA Rule 2090 (Know Your Customer) and FINRA Rule 2111 (Suitability). These rules were introduced with the filing of SR-FINRA-2010-039 and went into effect on July 12, 2012.

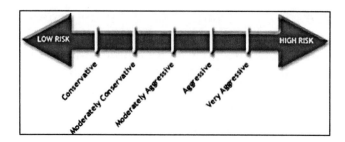

Determining an investor's ideal risk level involves assessing and combining financial goals, personal perspective and comfort, amount invested and the realities of the financial markets such as market volatility and outlook. Only one option should be selected from the risk tolerance scale.

When determining investment objectives, the broker dealer must take into account the investor's age, other investments, income and financial needs, tax status, risk tolerance, time horizon, liquidity needs, and any other information the investor chooses to disclose. Examples of investment objectives to select from include:

> Liquidity   > Capital Preservation
> Capital Appreciation   > Conservative
> Tax free/deferral   > Speculation
> Income   > Growth

Cross out "speculation" unless you are truly comfortable with the possibility of losing most, or all, of your money. The financial advisor will use this information, combined with risk tolerance, as the basis for investment recommendations. This is the most important part of the account agreement and needs to be carefully considered. Brokerage firms are accountable for any strategy they may recommend to the client based upon the client's stated circumstances and objectives. Therefore, it is extremely important that the information disclosed by the customer be complete, accurate and up to date. Accountability does not mean, however, that a brokerage firm will easily own up to any shortcomings in their duties. Should a dispute arise against a firm from a customer, all information provided, or lack thereof, will be used by the brokerage firm in defending itself. Brokers often encourage clients to check all boxes. If there is an investment objective that should not be included, it should be crossed out. If all of the options are checked, or left blank, the broker will assign each selection equal weight. When checking the options, it is best to rank the options in order of preference and cross out any that should not be included.

The customer must be proactive in disclosing to the brokerage firm the maximum amount of information related to their account. This will be the customer's greatest protection to defend themselves against the brokerage firm should a dispute arise. If any circumstances change in the customer's life, it is important to contact the firm and update the financial profile each time. It may take a few minutes, but those minutes could help save years of heartache and frustration. Periodically, the investment firms will send out letters asking if the investment objectives are still accurate. Pay careful attention to these letters and return them to the firm, but only after reading and responding to them accurately.

There are many options to choose from when selecting investment objectives and risk tolerance. The following chart briefly describes terms that every investor should understand in order to complete a brokerage account opening application:

Risk Tolerance Definitions:

Conservative	Investor is willing to accept the lowest fluctuation in account value in exchange for the lowest return possible.
Conservative/Moderate	Investor is willing to accept a relatively low fluctuation in account value in exchange for a below average return potential.
Moderate	Investor is willing to accept an average fluctuation in account value in exchange for an average return potential
Moderate/Aggressive	Investor is willing to accept a relatively high fluctuation in account value in exchange for a high return potential.
Aggressive	Investor is willing to accept the highest fluctuation in account value in exchange for the highest return potential.

Investment Objective Definitions:

Capital Preservation Conservative	The primary goal is preservation of capital over growth or income.
Income	The primary goal is income provided by the investment (e.g. dividends) rather than growth potential.
Tax Considerations	The primary investment goal is investments that mitigate federal, state and/or local taxes.
Protection	The primary goal is leaving a monetary benefit at death to loved ones or charity.
Education	The primary goal is paying for education related expenses.
Estate Planning	The primary goal is transferring assets to loved ones and/or providing a legacy at one's death.
Growth	The primary goal is an increase in the capital or market value of the investment rather than income that may be received from the investment.
Speculation	The primary goal requires an acceptance of higher than average risk and/or loss of capital in hope of making a higher than average return. Note: Investors should realize that what this really means is that they must be willing to risk everything in pursuit of a higher return.

If a firm's account application does not provide a thorough list of options to select from for both investment objectives and risk tolerance, the firm is not requesting enough information from its customers. It is a questionable practice if a firm fails to request a customer's risk tolerance, but some do not request this information for all types of brokerage accounts. Ask for an opportunity to provide additional information about investment objectives and risk tolerance if it is not requested. If the firm refuses to allow customers to be more specific, be very suspicious and seriously consider going somewhere else. For an investor to successfully counter a firm's defenses, all critical information regarding the investor's goals and objectives need to be complete, accurate, up to date, and in writing.

D. Investment Experience:

To their own detriment, investors are often inclined to declare themselves to be more experienced than they actually are. A customer's investment experience is only used by the firm to remove responsibility for poor investment advice and shift it back to the customer. An investor's previous experience provides the broker no insight or information about the customer for determining what kind of investments to recommend. Don't overstate investment savvy or speculation.

BusinessDictionary.com defines a sophisticated investor as one who "**has sufficient experience and knowledge of the financial markets, and is able to evaluate a particular investment on its merits.**" It is common for someone to check a box that demonstrates 20 years of investing in mutual funds because that is how long they have had a 401(k) account. In an extreme example, during FINRA arbitration, one brokerage firm used a customer's investment experience in its own defense to say that the customer was a very sophisticated investor. Her new account form stated that she had 60 years of investment experience. The woman was 100 years old!

Declaring one's investment savvy on the account application only serves the purpose of helping the brokerage firm defend itself against accusations of wrongdoing. If a customer is opening an account at a full service brokerage firm, presumably, it is because that person intends to rely on the expertise of the financial advisors.

E. How to Manage Un-invested Cash:

Oftentimes there is cash in an account that hasn't been invested. For example, there may have been a deposit into an account without instructions on how to invest it, or cash may be deposited as a result of cash dividends or interest. The brokerage firm typically will automatically place, or "sweep," that cash into a cash management program ("cash sweep" program).

On a new account application, the brokerage firm may ask the investor to select a cash management program. Cash management programs offer different benefits and risks, including different interest rates and insurance coverage. Be sure to understand the different features of the cash management programs that the firm offers so that you can make an informed decision if asked to choose one.

F. Contractual Provisions:

Keep in mind that the fine print in this agreement was drafted by the brokerage firm for its own protection. Read and understand every paragraph before signing this contract. Ask for clarification if there is any word, sentence, paragraph or detail that you do not understand.

a) <u>Arbitration Agreement</u>: This section is where the customer waives their right to have any potential dispute tried in court. Every brokerage firm inserts this paragraph into their account agreements. It commits the customers to FINRA arbitration. Anyone who opens a brokerage account has no other choice. Again, this provision is for the benefit of the brokerage firm, not the customer. Be aware that investors, by signing this agreement, waive all rights to pursue remedies in court.

b) <u>Suitability</u>: Charles Schwab includes the following language in the fine print of their account agreements:

> "I acknowledge that I am responsible for determining the nature, potential value and suitability for me of any particular security, transaction, or investment strategy and that Schwab does not give legal or tax advice or advice regarding particular stocks, including advice involving suitability of and investment strategies for particular stocks."

c) **Attorney's Fee Provision:** The authors are aware of only one firm which has a clause calling for attorney's fees to be paid by a Claimant who loses a case in arbitration. Imagine the appalling situation. Investors win only approximately 44% of cases they bring in arbitration. When they win, they get only between 12% - 37%, depending on the size of the claim because larger claims historically receive a smaller percentage, of what they lost. They are not able to go to a court but are required, under the terms of the agreement, to seek arbitration. Now, at least one firm requires the client to pay attorney's fees should they lose the case.

Our advice to any and all investors is simple and straight forward. Ask the firm you are opening an account with if such a clause is a part of their account opening agreement. Get their response and read the document carefully to be sure you are being given accurate information. If such a clause exists, then ask for one of two remedies. Either tell them to strike and initial that clause from the agreement or immediately tell the broker that you will be taking your account and business elsewhere if that clause is not removed.

This type of language should never be found in the agreement of any firm that provides any investment advice or recommendations. This type of language should only be found in agreements where all transactions are self-directed. Check the agreement carefully for any language that absolves the brokerage firm of responsibility.

If you give the power of information away to your broker, it can be used against you. Take a hands-on approach when it comes to taking care of your investments. The business model of the securities industry is anchored in the philosophy of the brokerage firms making money, not in protecting investors. It is critical to provide, in writing, everything expected from your investment account and your brokerage firm. Take the time to determine what investment objectives and risk tolerance are right for you. Do not let the brokerage firms make those decisions. In most arbitration cases, the first exhibit presented by the defense is the account opening agreement.

Key Points:
➢ Never sign a blank agreement.
➢ Understand every paragraph of the account opening documents before signing.
➢ Always provide complete and accurate information when opening an account.
➢ Remember that your broker is first, and foremost, a salesman.
➢ Broker dealers will not take responsibility for your losses unless they are forced to do so.

Avoid losses in the first place. Recovery is much more difficult than avoidance.

***

HORROR STORY

A medical practitioner had been through a difficult divorce. A patient of his suggested that he could recoup some of his losses by starting a commodities trading account. The results were disastrous and, in this case, very likely fatal.

In only four months, the doctor lost over $1.5 Million. Commissions charged by the brokerage firm during the four month period were over $1.75 Million, which EXCEEDED total losses by more than $200,000. In other words, his losses were not a function of the market. There was a 950% cost to average equity ratio and an annualized turnover rate of 36.20 in the account. Normally, a turnover of anything over 6 is presumed to be churning. The costs extracted from the account amounted to a transfer of the doctor's net worth from his retirement account into the account of the brokerage firm.

An action was brought before a National Futures Association (NFA) arbitration panel. As with FINRA members, clients do not have the option of bringing an action in court but, instead, are at the mercy of NFA arbitration panels. Under the applicable rules there are no fiduciary duties and the suitability standards of FINRA do not even exist in the NFA world.

The case went to arbitration and the investor was found to have knowingly taken the risk and that all commissions were "reasonable."

The doctor, knowing he could never recover his losses, suffered a heart attack soon thereafter and died.

***

<u>Churning</u>

The investment landscape is littered with stories of investors whose accounts have been churned into oblivion. In a recent case investigated by the authors, a broker dealer generated commissions equal to 50% of the value of the account in a period of less than 90 days. The victims were elderly and the abuse was not discovered until their son reviewed their account and realized what had been done. Sadly, this is not an isolated event.

Churning a customer's account is one of the most insidious forms of abuse which occurs at Wall Street brokerage houses. Churning occurs when a broker, exercising control over the volume and frequency of trading, abuses his customer's confidence for personal gain. This is done by initiating transactions that are excessive in view of the character of the account. A broker who "churns" a customer's account is considered to breach his fiduciary duty to his customer by acting for his own interests and disregarding the interests of the customer.

A broker is generally compensated for the volume of transactions that he executes for a customer. This often motivates a broker to execute trades on behalf of customers that are excessive in light of the objectives and resources of the customer's account.

A churning claim does not focus on the impropriety of a particular transaction, or even a group of transactions, but rather, on the overall amount of trading which is alleged to be excessive in view of the size and character of the account.

In order to establish a claim for churning, a customer must prove three elements: (1) that the trading in his account was excessive in light of his investment objectives; (2) that the broker in question exercised control over the trading and account; and (3) that the broker acted with the intent to defraud, or with the willful and reckless disregard for the interest of the client (also known as scienter).

There is no universal formula for evaluating whether churning has occurred in an account. However, the analysis generally starts with an examination of the volume and frequency of the transactions in light of the nature of the account and the situation, i.e., needs and objectives of the customer. The critical issue is whether the volume of transactions, when considered in light of the nature and objectives of the account, was so excessive as to indicate a purpose on the part of the broker to derive a profit for himself at the expense of his customer.

The most commonly used measure of excessiveness is the turnover ratio. Generally, the turnover ratio is computed by dividing the total dollar value of purchases (but not sales) made for an account during a particular period by the average equity (total amount invested, less margin debt) in the account during that period. The turnover ratio affords the opportunity to determine how many times in a given period the securities in a customer's account have been replaced by new securities. However, whether or not a particular turnover ratio is excessive depends on the objectives of the particular customer, as each customer is unique and may have different investment objectives.

While there is no ratio that is universally recognized as being determinative of churning, an annual turnover ratio of six times is considered to raise a presumption of excessive trading. There have

[22]

been situations where a finding of churning was upheld even though the turnover ratio was less than six.

Another method for measuring excess activity is by calculating the cost to equity ratio. This test analyzes the relationship between the net amount of money invested and the transaction costs that are incurred. The cost to equity ratio is computed by dividing the total fees, commissions, markups, markdowns, margin interest, etc. during a particular period by the average equity in the account and then annualizing the result. The higher the cost to equity ratio is, the stronger the case that can be made for excessive trading.

Analysis of an account to determine if churning has occurred can also be done by looking at the nature of the trading in the account. A pattern of trading that furthers the broker's interest in generating commissions, without offering an appropriate benefit to the customer, is also strong evidence of churning. Churning is often referred to as "in and out trading" which has been defined as "a sale of all or part of the customer's portfolio with the proceeds immediately reinvested in other securities followed, in a short period, by the sale of the newly acquired securities."

Cross trading can also be a pattern of trading which reflects that an account has been churned. Cross trading occurs when a broker arranges for transfers between customers. It is considered to be a highly suspect practice, unless the dealer can demonstrate that the accounts had different purposes and that the particular securities were suitable for one account but not another. Again, depending upon the type of account being traded and the objectives of the customer, the analysis for excessive trading will be different.

Control of trading is an essential element of churning. An issue of control is generally a question of fact that depends on all the circumstances surrounding each particular case. Of course, control by the broker can be satisfied if the customer has given the broker discretionary authority to initiate transactions on their behalf. However, even in the absence of an express argument, control may be inferred from the broker-customer relationship when the customer lacks the ability to manage the account and historically has taken the broker's word for what is happening. Conversely, a customer may be deemed to have retained control of his account if he has sufficient financial acumen to determine his own best interest and he acquiesces in the broker's handling of the account.

Even when the broker does not have <u>actual</u> authority to control the customer's account, he may obtain what is referred to as *de facto* control. Arbitrators consider several factors in determining whether the broker exercised *de facto* control over an account, such as: (1) lack of customer sophistication; (2) lack of prior trading experience on the part of the customer; (3) minimum amount of time devoted by the customer to the account; (4) high degree of trust and confidence placed in the broker by the customer; (5) large percentage of transactions entered into by the customer based upon the broker's recommendation; (6) absence of prior customer approval for transactions entered into on his behalf; and (7) customer's approval of recommended transactions where approval is not based upon fully truthful and accurate information. In addition, the customer's age, education and financial expertise, as well as the broker-client relationship, may be considered.

The final element that must be established in proving that a customer's account has been churned is that the broker acted with scienter.

The United States Supreme Court has stated that scienter is "a mental state embracing intent to deceive, manipulate, or defraud." <u>El Rizek v. SEC</u>, 215 F.3d 157 (1st Cir. 2000). An investor is not required to show actual intent on the part of the broker. Some courts have accepted a reckless disregard for the interest of the customer as a substitute. Additionally, scienter may be established by looking at the overall scheme or conduct of the broker in dealing with the customer's account; it is not necessary to establish a specific intent to defraud as to each trade executed. In a churning case, scienter may be inferred from the broker's conduct since churning, in and of itself, may be considered a deceptive and manipulative device in violation of federal and state securities laws.

In recognizing that the amount of actual damages sustained as a result of churning is often difficult to calculate, both arbitration panels and courts have continuously held that some uncertainty of damages should not work to bar a customer from recovering against the broker. Moreover, an investor who has been the victim of churning is entitled to excess commissions even if the account made a profit, and the guilty broker dealer is <u>not</u> entitled to offset commissions by that profit. In churning cases, an abused investor may also be entitled to punitive damages given the egregious nature of the activity.

Key Points:
➢ Track activity in your account.
➢ Don't provide discretionary authority.
➢ Periodically check on the turnover ratio and cost to equity ratio in your account.

Using False Assumptions to Lure Retirees

Employees have been provided with the opportunity to retire early and take funds out of their retirement accounts without paying the 10% early penalty withdrawal. This is made possible by an Internal Revenue Service (IRS) provision at Section 72(t).

The employee can take an early retirement and then roll their 401(k) into an IRA. After the rollover is completed, the employee can apply for a 72(t) "equally substantial distribution." The IRS offers three optional payment methods: minimum distribution, amortization and annuitization.

The chance to grasp these often sizeable sums of investment dollars from large groups of employees of major corporations has proved to be an irresistible siren song for many on Wall Street.

The firms often make overly aggressive assumptions while painting pictures of a leisurely retirement on sandy beaches. This is often done at seminars held at luxury hotels or even at the employer's offices where all those nearing retirement are invited. The one source investors should avoid in seeking important retirement advice is anyone affiliated with a brokerage firm. When the brokerage firm's assumptions prove to be disastrous over-estimations of return, the retirees are left with no job, greatly reduced investments and bleak retirement expectations.

It is important to understand the basics of the program. Once the rollover is completed and a 72(t) is set up to pay out a cash flow to the investor, it must continue, nonstop, until the age of 59½ or for a minimum of 5 years, whichever comes latest. If you set up a 72(t) at the age of 57, it must run until you are 62. If you are 50 at retirement, it must run until you are 59½. There is a cautionary tale to this program because once you set the 72(t) in motion you cannot change it. The plan must continue according to the actuarial tables, the time period selected and the distribution based on whichever of the three payment methods was chosen.

An early retiree who hires a broker to set up and invest his qualified retirement money is often provided with evidence that investors historically make 10% a year by investing in the stock market. The broker often fails to discuss the risks of the actual investments suggested to the early retiree. The combination of misleading income information coupled with a broker's failure to identify costs, expenses, and what happens when the stock market declines, is a serious problem.

Once the 72(t) has stopped payouts, the investor may take out any remaining amount in the account subject to being taxable at the then applicable tax rate. Using the 72(t) would have allowed avoidance of the 10% early withdrawal penalty.

If too much is withdrawn, the investor may well exhaust financial support and still have to face the IRS 10% early withdrawal penalty. In other words, if you force money out of the 72(t) account before it is scheduled, you may be assessed the 10% penalty you have sought to avoid.

It is extremely important that you work with a tax professional before setting up or utilizing a 72(t) distribution. Use caution because not all financial advisors, CPAs, or attorneys know and understand the requirements of Rule 72(t).

Brokerage firms often sell Variable Rate Annuities (VRAs) to 72(t) participants, not because of the desirability of the product for the retirees but, because of the large fees paid to the broker. A portion of that substantial fee is for the tax deferral benefit of a VRA. This represents a needless duplication in an already tax deferred account such as an IRA. As will be discussed later, VRAs are a great product for selling but not a good product for buying, especially in a tax deferred retirement account.

The 72(t) program can be a useful planning tool but it is only as good as the investments selected for the account. Don't be misled by "too good to be true" projections. Seek competent, independent advice both for setting up the structure and for selecting the investments which will enhance, rather than denigrate or destroy, a long-anticipated retirement.

Key Points:
➢ Don't accept 72(t) advice from a brokerage firm.
➢ Be certain that all withdrawals comply with applicable rules.
➢ Don't allow tax deferred products to be placed in a tax deferred account.

***
HORROR STORY
An elderly couple had successfully farmed their land in the Mississippi Delta for 50 years. It was hard work, hot work and very blue collar work. The hard working couple had successfully skimped, saved and invested their money with the local office of a Wall Street brokerage firm. Their broker placed their funds in a

discretionary account and made all investment selections, assuring them that he was relying on "experts" within his firm.

Within a few years, Bob and Jean lost $750,000 following the direct and specific advice of their broker. The broker spoke with them weekly, came to their house monthly and repeatedly told them that the mounting losses in their account were market driven and simply part of their risk as investors. This happened during years when the S&P increased over 100%.

The truth was that they were sold proprietary products, created and distributed, by their broker's firm. They never made any investment decisions on their own. They relied totally on selections made by the broker. The naïve couple believed hard work and a trusted financial advisor would pay off for them. Actually, the hard work did pay off for them. They were very successful in their farming operation for 50 years. Now in their late 70s, their investment losses wiped out all but $100,000 of the $850,000 invested with their broker, a neighbor and a friend.

After consulting a securities arbitration attorney, at the insistence of their son, the couple learned that the market was not responsible for their losses. They had been sold highly risky, proprietary limited partnerships that were wholly unsuitable for them. The elderly couple felt personally devastated when they learned that their broker and his firm had omitted to provide all types of important information to them when recommending proprietary investments. There was also a total failure to supervise.

The arbitration conducted under the auspices of FINRA Dispute Resolution took place in Memphis, Tennessee. The arbitrators ruled that all losses were the fault of these elderly farmers. There was, as is usual in FINRA arbitrations, no explanation for the award. As is often true in FINRA arbitrations, the three panelists all had long track records of ruling against claimants in over 80% of the cases they had heard.

The two hard working Americans were not only defrauded out of their life's savings by the Wall Street brokerage house but, adding insult to injury, they were ordered to pay an additional $12,000 towards arbitration expenses.

* * *

Seeking Discretionary Accounts

Individual investors should avoid actively managed discretionary accounts offered by broker dealers. In today's market place, managed accounts are all the rage for a number of reasons. Commissions and spreads on products have contracted substantially. There's a lot more transparency than there has been in the past. As a result, the profitability of firms has been cut and they've had to seek fertile ground for profitability elsewhere. One of the places they've gone to harvest that profitability is in the fields of discretionary accounts. Brokers are rewarded by their firms, in large part, by the number of dollars the broker has "under management." The incessant drive to "gather funds" is the chief motivating factor within almost every retail brokerage office in America.

In a typical situation, the broker convinces the customer that they are better off by having a "professional manager." The brokerage firm then charges a fee for selecting that manager and charges an ongoing fee for providing oversight of the manager's performance. In the event that the manager performs poorly, they then charge a fee for finding a replacement and blame the manager, certainly not themselves, for poor performance.

The trades that the manager does in the account are typically done through the brokerage firm that has selected the manager, which adds additional income to the broker's bottom line. This is often hidden under a number of subterfuges on the part of the brokerage firm. They often tell the clients that there are no charges other than the fees paid to have the funds managed. This simply is not true.

Some of the funds are managed internally by the brokerage firm's own proprietary managers. However, the vast majority are handled by outside managers because this provides more fee opportunities, less blame, and the perfect target to download excuses for poor performance. Typically, the brokerage firm is the first to get in line to get accolades thrown at them when the market goes up and the portfolio performs well. However, if there's a market downturn and the funds cease to perform as hoped, the firm then has the outside party to blame and, incredibly, can get a fee for removing, replacing and continuing to supervise the same dollars. The winner in all of this is the brokerage firm. The loser in all of this is the customer. There are virtually no situations in which this type of arrangement is the best financial situation for a customer to enter into. Avoid discretionary accounts.

Another reason for avoiding these types of accounts is that they are almost always actively managed. The historical numbers are overwhelming. The passively managed fund outperforms the active funds, generally, by at least the amount of difference in costs and many times by a substantially larger factor.

The bottom line again is, avoid actively managed discretionary accounts.

Key Points:
➢ Don't agree to a discretionary account with a brokerage firm.
➢ Open a discretionary account only through an independent advisor.
➢ Use only passively managed funds.

***

HORROR STORY
A married couple, both of whom were in their late 80s, was persuaded by their bank to take out a 100% value equity line of credit against their home. They were then persuaded to turn these "borrowed assets" over to the bank's securities subsidiary where they were told the return would easily exceed the cost of the credit line.

The broker then advised the couple to put 95% of the total proceeds into a single stock. The securities account tanked, resulting in an almost 100% loss. In the meantime, the house dropped in value by $100,000, resulting in a foreclosure proceeding. The bank then refused to permit a $150,000 short sale to bona fide buyers.

The husband died. The wife, who now lives in a constant care facility, is entering bankruptcy to force the bank to take the house.

Of course, the bank and their securities subsidiary blame it all on the elderly couple whom they described as "sophisticated investors." Both husband and wife had been school teachers and had no training or experience in the securities industry or in investment strategies. The fact that both were in their late 80s and suffering from diminished capacity, was not enough to deter the aggressive sales tactics of their "trusted advisors."

***

Playing the Market with Your Home Equity

Americans often see the equity in their homes as sacrosanct, but occasionally a broker, looking for a commission, will talk homeowners into mortgaging their home to buy securities. It is almost certainly inappropriate and something an investor should never agree to do.

This was a fashionable lure used by many brokerage houses prior to the real estate price drops of 2007. Some brokers are attempting to resurrect the strategy now in areas where real estate suffered smaller losses and/or may be staging a slight recovery. Don't fall for it!

Rising stock markets and falling interest rates are generally a good thing for all concerned. However, this combination of positive factors, especially when combined with large gains in home prices, led to reckless actions by some investors and unsuitable sales practices by investment professionals.

This is actually one area where FINRA provided helpful guidance prior to the strategy which destroyed so many lives.

The National Association of Securities Dealers (NASD), now FINRA, was concerned enough about this dangerous practice to issue an Investor Alert, entitled <u>Betting the Ranch: Risking Your Home to Buy Securities</u>, in March 2004. That's right, 2004.

The NASD stated the reason for the Alert:

> NASD is issuing this alert because we are concerned that investors who must rely on investment returns to make their mortgage payments could end up defaulting on their home loans if their investments decline and they are unable to meet their monthly mortgage payments. In short, investors who bet the ranch could lose it.

This was a more accurate prediction than those made by Nostradamus!

The NASD recognized in the same Investor Alert that there is principal risk in "virtually any security." The Investor Alert went on to stress that borrowing against the equity in one's home to buy securities compounds the risk because:

> When you buy securities with mortgage money, you are investing with borrowed funds. While this increases your buying power, it also increases your exposure to market risk, similar to buying securities on margin. The difference is your mortgage loan is likely to be greater than any amount a securities firm would loan you on margin. Investing borrowed mortgage money amounts to a huge bet that the investment will increase.
>
> Unlike investing with savings, when you invest with mortgage money, you stand to lose more than your principal if the investment goes sour. You can lose the collateral supporting the loan – namely your house. Even if you don't lose your

house, you could lose the equity in your home that may have built up over a considerable period of time.

You may put your money in higher risk investments than you might normally select, in an effort not only to match the rate of your home loan but in the hopes of surpassing this rate. Furthermore, with so much at stake, if a given investment does poorly, you may feel compelled to move your investment into even more risky investments to make up the difference, further jeopardizing your home, credit standing, and overall financial health.

Of course, most investors do not "select" investments. Far more investments are sold to investors by broker dealers than are purchased or selected by investors.

The NASD offered a real-life scenario to illustrate the danger, a scenario that has become a nightmare for many investors:

Worst Case Scenarios Can Happen

NASD is aware of the instances in which investors have had difficulties paying their mortgages as a result of declines in their mortgage-financed investments. Here's how this can happen:

A retired couple's house is paid off, but they have very little extra money to meet their everyday living expenses. They decide to take out a new mortgage of $250,000 at 6%, seeking to invest this mortgage money in the hope of making more than 6%. They lock into a mortgage requiring monthly payments of $1,663. On the advice of their broker, they invest their mortgage money in a mutual fund that has earned an average of 12% over the past five years. But instead of gaining value, the couple's investment loses money from the start and continues to decline. After one year, their investment is worth $200,000. Since they were depending on this investment to generate $1,663 per month to pay the loan and have no other assets to liquidate to make up the difference, they are faced with a tough choice: sell off part of their now depleted original investment to pay the mortgage payments and hope that the investment turns around, or sell their house and hope that the selling price is enough to pay off the loan and pay for real estate commissions. Either way, they run the risk of losing money – and their home.

In December 2004, the NASD again expressed concern over this problem when Notice to Members[2] (NTM) 04-89, entitled Liquefied Home Equity, was issued. The NASD noted that it was alerting members to "concerns when recommending or facilitating investments of liquefied home equity." The NTM offered an excellent summary of the problem:

Executive Summary

The rapid increase in home prices over the past several years, in combination with refinancing activity by homeowners, has led to increasing investment activity by homeowners with equity from their homes. This *Notice* reminds members that recommending liquefying home equity to purchase securities may not be suitable for all investors and that members, and their associated persons, should perform a careful analysis to determine whether liquefying home equity is a suitable strategy for an investor. In addition,

---

[2] FINRA's Regulatory Notices were formerly known as Notice to Members. FINRA describes Regulatory Notices as communications to member firms which discuss FINRA rules including notice of recently approved rules and amendments, proposed rules on which FINRA is soliciting comment, and legal interpretations and guidance relating to existing rules. Regulatory Notices may also address rules of the Securities and Exchange Commission (SEC) or other governmental agencies. FINRA members, in hearings, often take the position that NTMs are only "advice" and they can choose to ignore them.

members should ensure that all communications with the public addressing a strategy of liquefying home equity are fair and balanced, and accurately depict the risks of investing with liquefied home equity. Finally, members should consider whether to employ heightened scrutiny of accounts that they know, or have reason to know, are funded with liquefied home equity.

While the idea of earning some sort of return on your home equity is appealing, that thought should be countered <u>by the risk of losing your home to foreclosure</u>. There are incredible risks to using home equity as a pool of money to invest in the stock market.

First, investors are not guaranteed a 10% return as many brokers will tell you the stock market has produced historically. Investors do lose money in the stock market as seen by numerous financial crises and by precipitous drops in individual stocks even in favorable market conditions. Sure, your money might return 10%. It also might return 200%. However, all investments are at risk for loss, so you might lose all of it, leaving you with nothing to pay off your home equity loan. You would literally be starting over on paying off your house, **IF** you had the financial ability to avoid losing the house.

Second, the cost of borrowing is a fixed cost that digs into any investment return that you might be getting. If you use your home equity, you will have to pay interest on the loan. If you use cash-out refinancing, you have to pay refinancing closing costs on top of interest on a larger loan. A cash-out refinancing might cost you thousands in closing costs. You would have to be extremely lucky to string together several years of gains to make a nice return on your investment.

Finally, you would be giving up the greater security of having equity in your house. You might think you are going to live in that house forever, but life's circumstances can be unpredictable. You may get a promotion three years later and find yourself in need of selling the home quickly.

[35]

Owning your home free and clear prior to retirement is a sound life goal. Tapping the equity in your home to invest in other assets, whether in stocks, bonds, commodities or other real estate investments, never makes sense if you have most of your wealth tied up in a home.

An investor should never borrow against their home to purchase securities. The risk is too great and the potential consequences too dire. The NASD offers the best advice to investors, just say no to betting the ranch to invest in securities. The corollary to that advice is to run as fast as possible from a broker advising you to follow such a "strategy."

Key Point:
> ➤ Never borrow against the value of your home and use the proceeds for other investments.

Brokers Often Allow Investors to Commit Financial Suicide

If you are in the deep end of the swimming pool and struggling to swim, does the lifeguard have an obligation to try to save you or can they just watch? A trained lifeguard must respond or be held liable for not trying. The same principal applies to your stockbroker. He cannot let you get in way over your head and, when he knows you are in danger, abandon you. A broker cannot allow you to commit financial suicide.

Even when an investor affirmatively seeks to engage in highly speculative or aggressive trading, a broker is under a duty to refrain from making recommendations that are incompatible with the customer's profile or to blindly fill orders while knowing the customer is committing financial suicide. Courts have held that a broker's responsibility goes beyond mechanical obedience to customer demands.

There are several cases which have dealt specifically with the subject of financial suicide.

Charles W. Eye, 50 S.E.C. 655, 658 (1991). **"Her request for a plan to increase that income was not a warrant to escalate risks unduly. If the only method capable of producing the desired income involved significant dangers, Eye should have been advised against it."**

District Business Conduct Committee v. Michael R Euripedes, No. C9B950014, (1994) NASD Discp. LEXIS 45 at *13 **" representative has consultative duty when customers wish to engage in trading that is inconsistent with their financial situation."**

Clyde J. Bruff, 50 S.E.C. 1266, 1269 (1992), **"having undertaken to act as an investment counselor for the Pattersons, Bruff was required to make only such recommendations in the best interests of his customer even when such recommendations contradict the customer's wishes."**

The usual brokerage firm defense was not accepted when an arbitration panel specifically rejected testimony from a Prudential expert that, "We were mere order takers." The Panel reasoned that even if the client directed all trading in his account, it would not excuse the broker from taking steps to prevent a financial suicide. Arbitration panels have consistently found that a broker has a fiduciary duty to take action when it is obvious a client is trading inappropriately, is losing large amounts of money, and is putting excessive amounts of net worth at risk.

When such circumstances arise, the broker dealer's compliance department has an obligation to contact the customer to determine what is happening, or to send a letter to the customer questioning the account activity and to follow up on the letter. The firm is obligated to maintain records showing that they took steps to prevent a financial suicide.

Ultimately, the firm may well be obligated to halt all trading and close the account.

It may seem unfair to a brokerage firm that they can be held liable for allowing a ruinous course of conduct by a willing investor making their own decisions about their own money. However, the analysis becomes more complex in most situations. For example, South Florida is home to a large number of retirees. As longevity increases, many elderly investors begin to suffer the ravages of dementia. The authors see many examples of heirs finding out after the death of a parent that the assets of their loved one were squandered in foolish trading permitted, or even encouraged, by a negligent or profit motivated broker who turned a blind eye to the activity.

The liability extended to brokers in this type of situation is no different than the standard imposed on bartenders, doctors writing prescriptions or many others who interact with customers or their own employees. A full service brokerage firm, which holds itself out as providing "financial advice" to its customers, cannot escape liability for its customer's acts of financial suicide by claiming that "we only sold him the bullets." The firm has a duty to intervene and stop an obviously disastrous course of trading, just like what is expected of lifeguards.

Key Point:
➤ Children should take reasonable steps to protect aging and infirm parents from improper account activity.

Portraying Bonds as Risk-Free Investments

Many investors are told that bonds are "safe." They are "risk free." You "can't lose your principal." These and other similar statements are made by sellers of fixed income investments. These statements and the perceptions they lead to are false and can lead to disastrous consequences. There is obviously great confusion in the mind of many investors. It is important to understand what is meant by the term "bonds" and to fully appreciate the risks involved in purchasing and holding various types of bonds.

The term "bond" is used to mean numerous types of debt securities. All bonds, just like all stocks, are not created "equal." If an investor purchases Treasury bills, notes or bonds, they are presumed to have no credit risk because the U.S. government would have to fail for the investor not to get back their principal. However, the purchaser of bonds issued by a non-rated corporation or public entity may well be exposed to the possibility of a default and the loss of the investor's principal.

As stated above, some investors have been erroneously led to believe that all "bonds" are safe. Not so. An investor is entitled to know the credit status and understand how to evaluate the degree of risk to which they are exposed in selecting a particular bond. This is known as credit risk, and a bad decision can lead to the loss of *all* of an investor's principal. Every bond must be evaluated separately and thoroughly for an investor to fully appreciate the embedded credit risk.

It is not within the scope of this book to do a detailed analysis of credit ratings. As we learned the hard way during the "credit crisis," the ratings assigned by the three primary ratings agencies (Moody's, Standard & Poor's and Fitch) were not dependable and remain suspect in any future crisis. They do serve as a basic guide, but an investor should not assume the ratings to be totally accurate and fully reflective of underlying risk. This startling fact is, in itself, enough to raise deep concerns in the mind of an investor who has been led to believe that they can rest easy by virtue of owning "bonds."

The basic meanings of the credit ratings of Moody's, Standard & Poor's and Fitch as shown in Wikipedia are set out below:

Bond Credit Rating

In investments, the bond credit rating assesses the credit worthiness of a corporation's debt issues. The credit rating is a financial indicator to potential investors of debt securities such as bonds. These are assigned by credit rating agencies such as Moody's, Standard & Poor's and Fitch to have letter designations (such as AAA, B, CC) which represent the quality of a bond.

Bond ratings below BBB-/Baa- are called junk bonds and are deemed to be non-investment grade (which means they may not be purchased by many regulated investors) or speculative.

Moody's		S&P		Fitch		
Long-term	Short-term	Long-term	Short-term	Long-term	Short-term	
Aaa	P-1	AAA	A-1+	AAA	F1+	Prime
Aa1		AA+		AA+		High grade
Aa2		AA		AA		
Aa3		AA-		AA-		
A1		A+	A-1	A+	F1	Upper medium grade
A2		A		A		
A3	P-2	A-	A-2	A-	F2	
Baa1		BBB+		BBB+		Lower medium grade
Baa2	P-3	BBB	A-3	BBB	F3	
Baa3		BBB-		BBB-		
Ba1		BB+		BB+		Non-investment grade speculative
Ba2		BB		BB		
Ba3		BB-	B	BB-	B	
B1		B+		B+		Highly speculative
B2		B		B		
B3		B-		B-		
Caa1	Not prime	CCC+				Substantial risks
Caa2		CCC				Extremely speculative
Caa3		CCC-	C	CCC	C	Default imminent with little prospect for recovery
Ca		CC				
		C				
C				DDD		In default
/		D	/	DD	/	
/				D		

Credit risk is just one of the risks to which investors are exposed. Another risk involves "spread." Investors should be aware that most bonds trade on spread, meaning the difference between the "bid" and "ask." The larger the spread the greater the difference between bid and ask and, therefore, the greater the risk. The greater the risk, generally, the greater the spread, which means the greater the incentive for a sales person to sell bonds which carry a higher default risk. Bonds rarely trade like stocks on a set "commission."

If a buyer needs to sell a bond purchased earlier and the bond has a substantial spread, the investor may be exposed to a loss, even though the "market" has not experienced price decreases.

Bonds are also subject to "call" risk. An issuer will often reserve the right to "call" bonds when market conditions favor the issuer. An investor may think their funds are locked into an attractive rate, only to find that the bonds are "called" and the investor is forced to reinvest at a much lower and less attractive rate of return. Few investors understand the "callable" risk, and few brokers bother to explain it properly, if at all.

The greatest risk of owning a bond other than credit risk is "interest rate" risk. The NASD was concerned enough about the risks of owning bonds to issue NTM 04-30, which dealt with Sales Practice Obligations. Much of the Notice dealt with interest-rate risk. The NASD noted that:

> "...study by NASD indicates that 60% of investors do not understand that, as interest rates rise, existing bond prices fall, and that long-term bonds are more exposed to interest-rate risk than short-term bonds." It is critical that any bond investor understand the relationship between a bond's value and interest rates. Remember, a bond is a debt investment and represents an obligation to pay a particular rate of interest to the holder of that bond.

[41]

If the bond is issued at 6% that means the issuer is obligated to pay 6% to the holder. At 6%, the bond is said to trade at "par." However, if interest rates go up, investors will want a higher rate of interest on their bond investments. A purchaser in the secondary market will only buy the 6% bond if it is offered at a discount, meaning at a price below par, which would represent a loss for the original purchaser if he is forced to sell. Interest rate risks are not as great as credit risks but can be devastating to those forced to sell into unfavorable market conditions. Even those bonds with the highest possible credit standing are subject to interest-rate risk.

Be aware, know and understand your risks as a bond investor. The NASD made clear in NTM 04-30 that a broker-dealer's sales practice obligations include:

> ➢ Understanding the terms, conditions, risks and rewards of bonds and bond funds they sell (performing a reasonable-basis suitability analysis);

> ➢ Making certain that a particular bond or bond fund is appropriate for a particular customer before recommending it to that customer (performing a customer-specific suitability analysis);

> ➢ Providing a balanced disclosure of the risks, costs and rewards associated with a particular bond or bond fund, especially when selling to retail investors;

> ➢ Adequately training and supervising employees who sell bonds and bond funds; and

> ➢ Implementing adequate supervisory controls to reasonably ensure compliance with NASD and SEC sales practice rules in connection with bonds and bond funds.

As an investor, be certain that your broker dealer is living up to the standards set by NTM 04-30. Be aware of all the risks that go into owning bonds and bond funds.

Key Points:
➢ Understand the risks that exist in owning bonds.
➢ Know that when rates go up, the value of fixed income securities go down.

***
HORROR STORY

Hugh and his wife are retired public school teachers. Hugh's father had passed away, leaving Hugh and his wife accounts at a local brokerage firm. The broker called, introduced himself and asked a few questions. He said he would be faxing some forms over for signatures to establish new accounts in the names of the beneficiaries. He said not to worry about filling them out, that he would use the information collected on the earlier phone call to fill in the information. Hugh and his wife received the forms, signed them and sent them back. After all, the broker had been working with Hugh's parents for years and Hugh remembered his father talking about what a great guy his broker was. Hugh gave the account application no further thought after that day. That proved to be a big mistake.

The broker had recommended some stocks and bonds as appropriate for the retired school teachers, but did not describe them in detail. He sent some prospectuses out, but as usual, Hugh placed them in a drawer and never read them. The broker had told him they were good investments, and Hugh knew the broker was much more knowledgeable than he. Also, Hugh knew he had been very emphatic with the broker, telling him that these funds were irreplaceable and he could not afford to lose a dime. Hugh opened a fee based account where the broker would make the trades and charge the account a percentage of the account balance, but there were to be no commissions on individual trades. The brokerage firm did not include the investment objectives on the account statements as many firms do. Hugh had no idea what the firm had on record for his investment objectives, and totally trusted the broker, his father's good friend.

At first, the broker kept a significant portion of the account in a money market. For about a year and a half, nothing changed in the account. Around that time, Hugh opened the account statements and noticed many transactions. His broker had never called him or discussed any trades, so he called the broker. Meanwhile, the account had lost over $140,000. The broker did not return repeated calls. Hugh finally asked the receptionist and was told that the broker had been let go a few months earlier. Hugh asked to speak to the branch manager but was told he was out. Hugh left word but did not get a return call. He then wrote a letter to the branch manager expressing concern about the losses.

The manager wrote back and said that the account documents showed "speculation" as an investment objective and that Hugh and his wife were willing to accept large fluctuations in exchange for growth opportunities. The letter stated:

> **"Please note that these investments were one component of an overall investment strategy for each of your accounts and your total liquid net worth. In addition, it appears the above-noted investments were consistent with your overall investment objectives. Neither your broker nor our firm can be held responsible for those circumstances which led to the downward price movement of the securities."**

Hugh lost over $142,000. After he received the letter from the firm, he asked for copies of his account documents. What he found was that the firm thought he was worth over $2,000,000 and that he apparently had an aggressive risk tolerance and was willing to take risk in exchange for higher returns. This is not at all what he discussed with his broker. Unfortunately for Hugh, the damage was done and the signed documents will make it very difficult to expect any meaningful recovery of his losses. Had he been diligent in filling out the account forms, and had he demanded and reviewed the completed documents, the entire problem might have been avoided. If the forms were not available to the firm to be used against them, Hugh and his wife might at least have been able to extract a reasonable settlement from the brokerage firm. Sadly, what happened to Hugh and his wife is not an isolated occurrence. It happens on a consistent basis. Don't let it happen to you!

***

Unauthorized Trading

Unauthorized trading involves the purchase or sale of securities in a customer's account without the customer's prior knowledge and authorization. For example, the broker may believe a transaction is in the investor's best interest but cannot, or does not, contact the investor and then makes the trade anyway. The broker may make a trade believing he can later convince the investor to ratify, or approve, the trade after the fact. Remember, brokers generate commissions through executing transactions (sales or purchases). Unauthorized trading is outright theft. Don't consider it to be anything less.

The only person who can place a trade is the OWNER of the account. A husband cannot place a trade in the wife's account or vice-versa.

In most cases, unauthorized trading is discovered through reading confirmations and regular account statements. This may occur when the customer receives a confirmation in the mail for an unknown trade. In many instances, these transactions involve existing assets in the account and do not require client payment. In some cases, an existing asset may be liquidated to fund the purchase of a new security. Failing to read trade confirmations or monthly statements provides a broker with the opportunity to trade an account without objection.

In order to avoid this problem, always repeat instructions to your broker to promote a clear mutual understanding of the transaction. Read and retain, in a timely fashion, your monthly account statements, confirmations, and any other information you receive about your investment transactions.

Finally, take **immediate** action if you see a transaction you do not recognize. **Time is critical**. Reconcile any discrepancies at once. Contact the firm's branch manager. Send an e-mail, registered or overnight letter to the compliance department of the firm refusing the purchase. Also, follow up with a phone call to the firm's compliance department. The longer the lag time, the less substance and credibility your argument has.

<u>Key Points:</u>
➤ Read trade confirmations and monthly statements.
➤ Never ratify an unauthorized transaction.

Chapter 2
More Ways Wall Street Rips Off Investors

Inappropriately Casting Non-Accredited Investors as Accredited Investors

A prospectus on a new offering by a brokerage house will often say "available only to accredited investors." The idea is to protect those who are unable to take the risk involved in the new offering. Unfortunately, today in FINRA arbitration this is used to hurt customers, not protect them.

Black's Law Dictionary offers both a definition and the impact on a securities issuer in dealing with an accredited investor:

> An investor treated under the Securities Act of 1933 as being knowledgeable and sophisticated about financial matters, especially because of an investor's large net worth. In a securities offering that is exempt from registration, an accredited investor (which can be a person or an entity) is not entitled to protection under the Act's disclosure provisions although the investor does keep its remedies for fraud.

The definition of an "accredited investor" is spelled out in much greater detail and with great specificity in the Securities Act of 1993 and includes entities other than individuals.

A Confidential Private Placement Memorandum will always have a section limiting the offering to "accredited investors." One example of this type disclaimer is set out below:

> This Memorandum does not constitute an offer to any person who is not an "accredited investor" as defined in Rule 501 under Regulation D promulgated under the Securities Act of 1933, as amended. In making an investment, prospective investors must rely on their examination of the

> Partnership and the Terms of the Offering. An investment in Partnership Interests is illiquid and involves a high degree of risk. Accordingly, each Prospective Investor should consult with their attorney, accountant and other professionals prior to making an investment.

It is important that investors be aware that private placement issuers are subject to "disclosure" requirements, not to requirements that the investment be worthwhile. The Private Placement Memorandum will typically inform "accredited investors" of the limits of the "disclosure" through language similar to that set out below:

> This Memorandum has not been filed with, or reviewed by, the Securities and Exchange Commission ("SEC") or any other federal or state commission or regulatory authority nor have any of the foregoing authorities determined whether it is accurate or complete or passed upon or endorsed the merits of this offering. Any representation to the contrary is unlawful.

It is crucial to understand; the sale to non-accredited investors could lead to a right of rescission (cancelling the sale and returning the full purchase price to the investor) on the part of the buyer and could also lead to the institution of enforcement proceedings against the issuer.

Despite clauses limiting the sale of private placements to "accredited" investors, the sale to 35 "non-accredited" investors is permitted under the rules. It is important to remember that "accredited" status does not automatically mean the securities are "suitable" for a particular investor. It is also true that sale to a "non-accredited" investor under the 35 investor exception does not mean that the sale to that investor is automatically "unsuitable." The suitability analysis is required as to investment objectives and other criteria regardless of the investor's status as "accredited" or "non-accredited."

[48]

Trouble often arises when a broker, desperate to make a sale, persuades an investor to "fill out the paperwork because it is just a formality." **"DO NOT EVER,"** sign a document inflating your net worth or elevating yourself to "accredited" status. It may be a temporary boost to your ego but may well have disastrous long-term consequences. The broker will argue that "you signed it" and he relied on you to be honest about your financial status. He likely will conveniently forget the assurances he made to you. Remember, in a "he said" versus "she said" confrontation, the paperwork will often be used to break the tie. Don't let your trust in "your friend, the broker" come back to haunt you.

Key Points:
➤ Don't falsely inflate your net worth to achieve "accredited" status.
➤ Being an "accredited" investor does not eliminate the requirement that investments sold to that investor be "suitable."

★★★
HORROR STORY
Miriam was in her 80s and had been a widow for 15 years. In 2007, at the suggestion of her broker, "a nice lady" she had "met at church," her entire life savings were turned over to a major broker dealer.

She filled out the account opening documents under the broker's direction. She did insist that her investment objective be shown as "conservative."

Despite the "conservative" objective, almost 100% of her funds were put into thinly traded, largely unknown stocks. Within 7 months, 75% of her savings were gone.

The brokerage firm denied any wrongdoing arguing that "it was the market" and that she "was an experienced and sophisticated investor."
★★★

Selling Unsuitable Products

Suitability claims represent the largest segment of actions brought by investors against broker dealers. FINRA focuses heavily on "suitability" in its arbitrator training. Compliance officers in brokerage firms place primary emphasis on monitoring the suitability of recommendations made by brokers. Even cases brought by investors alleging other types of wrongdoing often evolve into evaluations by arbitrators of the suitability of recommendations.

Given the concentration on this important area, after a lengthy study and evaluation process, FINRA has adopted new Suitability and Know Your Customer rules which took effect on July 12, 2012.

The new FINRA Suitability Rule (2111) replaces NASD Rule 2310 and FINRA Rule 2090. The Know Your Customer Rule replaces New York Stock Exchange (NYSE) Rule 405. Given the importance of both new rules, essential portions of the rules are set out below:

FINRA Rule 2111:

(a) A member or an associated person must have a reasonable basis to believe that a recommended transaction or investment strategy involving a security or securities is suitable for the customer, based on the information obtained through the reasonable diligence of the member or associated person to ascertain the customer's investment profile. A customer's investment profile includes, but is not limited to, the customer's age, other investments, financial situation and needs, tax status, investment objectives, investment experience, investment time horizon, liquidity needs, risk tolerance, and any other information the customer may disclose to the member or associated person in connection with such recommendation.

.03 Recommended Strategies. The phrase "investment strategy involving a security or securities" used in this Rule is to be interpreted broadly and would include, among other things, an explicit recommendation to hold a security or securities. However, the following communications are excluded from the coverage of Rule 2111 as long as they do not include (standing alone or in combination with other communications) a recommendation of a particular security or securities:

(a) General financial and investment information, including (i) basic investment concepts, such as risk and return, diversification, dollar cost averaging, compounded return, and tax deferred investment, (ii) historic differences in the return of asset classes (e.g., equities, bonds, or cash) based on standard market indices, (iii) effects of inflation, (iv) estimates of future retirement income needs, and (v) assessment of a customer's investment profile;

.05 Components of Suitability Obligations. Rule 2111 is composed of three main obligations: reasonable-basis suitability, customer-specific suitability, and quantitative suitability.

FINRA Rule 2090

Every member shall use reasonable diligence, in regard to the opening and maintenance of every account, to know (and retain) the essential facts concerning every customer and concerning the authority of each person acting on behalf of such customer.

.01 Essential Facts. For purposes of this Rule, facts "essential" to "knowing the customer" are those required to (a) effectively service the customer's account, (b) act in accordance with

any special handling instructions for the account, (c) understand the authority of each person acting on behalf of the customer, and (d) comply with applicable laws, regulations, and rules.

These rules do, if properly applied by regulators and arbitrators, provide expanded protection for investors.

Under the terms of the old NASD Rule 2310, a broker dealer was not supposed to recommend a security to a customer unless the broker dealer had a reasonable basis for believing that recommendation was suitable for the customer in light of the customer's financial situation and investment objectives.

This language obviously leaves much room for subjective reasoning and justification. An investor can see from the "flexibility" of the language, the need to be precise and complete in setting out both their financial situation and their <u>exact</u> investment objectives on all broker dealer forms and documentation.

The same advice to investors would apply when looking at the language of the former NYSE Rule 405:

NYSE Rule 405. Diligence as to Accounts

Every member organization is required through a principal executive or a person or persons designated under the provisions of Rule 342(b)(1) to (1) Use due diligence to learn the essential facts relative to every customer, every order, every cash or margin account accepted or carried by such organization and every person holding power of attorney over any account accepted or carried by such organization.

Under recently adopted FINRA Rule 2111 there are expanded and important suitability obligations which customers should expect broker dealers to be aware of and to follow. Broker dealers are still required to first perform a "reasonable basis suitability test" to determine if the product is suitable for any investor. This analysis has become increasingly important given the expanded sale of exotic and complex structured finance products.

In addition, the broker dealer is required to perform a suitability analysis for each customer transaction. The broker dealers also have an additional obligation to do a suitability analysis for each customer in connection with a "transaction or investment strategy involving a security or securities." FINRA has made clear that this requirement extends to a "recommendation to hold." This requirement did not exist under the old rule.

Broker dealers have consistently urged many investors to "stay the course," especially in the case of structured finance securities funds containing complex holdings which pay substantial trailing fees to brokers. It hits the brokers in the pocketbook when owners of these funds sell.

Rule 2111 also reduces some of the subjectivity in the broker dealer's use of "reasonable efforts" to gather information about the customer. The new Rule, as shown above, and FINRA Regulatory Notice 11-25, both call for a more specific gathering of facts.

Regulatory Notice 11-25 also informed firms that investment profiles could not be borrowed from one customer account and applied to another of the customer's accounts which might have different objectives:

> ... a firm should evidence the customer's intent to use different investment profiles or investment profile factors for the different account.

If you, as an investor, have different investment objectives for separate accounts, be sure that the broker is aware and be certain that your written account documents reflect those differences.

Customers are even more strongly advised than under the old rules to protect themselves by providing complete and accurate information. A valid customer claim can easily be undone if the broker dealer can demonstrate a lack of total candor on the part of the customer.

The new rules may well lead to increased enforcement actions by FINRA. This remains to be seen. Given past history, it is doubtful that the new rules will provide much comfort for abused investors subject to the whims of FINRA dispute resolution arbitration panels.

The main line of defense for investors is to protect themselves before a problem ever arises. If you insist on having an account with a FINRA registered broker dealer, be sure to take seriously your obligations of providing full and accurate information. Monitor and update the broker dealer with any changes in your personal or financial situation. Read any correspondence from the broker dealer to be sure that you are not waiving or forfeiting any protections or defenses.

Key Points:
➤ Be sure all investments in your account meet your written investment objectives.
➤ Always provide complete and accurate information.

∗∗∗

HORROR STORY

Linda, while working at a local telephone company, met a registered representative in the securities business. As a novice with no investments to her name other than the accumulated savings at her company, Linda wanted help to preserve her savings and plan for her upcoming retirement. Linda attended several retirement seminars hosted by her company, but had not yet made a decision on where she would be placing her money when she officially retired.

Linda went to an investment seminar held by a brokerage firm and, afterwards, Linda met with a broker. Linda gave the brokerage house two checks totaling approximately $490,000. She was told that the money would all be invested in stocks because "they had historically returned 10% a year." There was no allocation to any other type of assets. For six months, Linda received monthly statements from the brokerage house.

Although Linda looked at the monthly statements, she did not fully understand them. She was able to determine that she had not made much money during this time frame. As her monthly statements continued to arrive, she saw that the principal value of her accounts continued to go down. She asked the broker about her accounts and the broker would say: "Let's ride it out, the market always performs well over time."

Linda was never advised to put stop loss orders in her account. She relied on the broker who kept telling her that the market was "going to go back up" and that she would "make plenty of money to use for her retirement." As a professional hired to help her with her investment portfolio, Linda thought the broker's advice was sound and trustworthy.

As her holdings continued to go down, Linda made regular phone calls to her broker asking what was going on. He kept saying: "Ride it out."

Linda's husband began to look at her monthly statements and became alarmed about the amount of fees the broker was making off the trades in her account. He and Linda both met with the broker, in person, at least twice. The broker reassured them that the remaining principal in her account was "not in any danger." The second meeting was to have Linda sign papers to move her account from the broker's former employer to his new employer.

Then, a few months later, the broker disclosed to Linda that her account had performed worse than any other account he handled. The broker then came up with a "Top 20 stock portfolio" that he said would help bring Linda's account up in value. The portfolio was, again, all equities with no fixed-income holdings. Her losses mounted.

Linda continued to call the broker, but was getting desperate and began to ask if her remaining principal could be put in safer investments. It was at this point that the broker told Linda she was "stupid" for asking or suggesting such a thing. A few more months passed and the broker called Linda and told her that she needed to quit her part time job and get a full time job paying at least $35,000 per year because "she had lost so much money." Linda moved her account, but it cost Linda $600 to close the 20-stock portfolio due to commissions on each trade before the money got moved into the Money Market Fund account.

By the time all the costs were counted along with the losses, Linda's $490,000 in irreplaceable retirement funds had become worth less than $100,000.

***

Failing to Create Proper Asset Allocations

Most Wall Street firms talk a lot about proper asset allocations. Their ads often tout their commitment to the process of proper asset allocation. Unfortunately, the verbiage is often used to entice customers. However, once enticed into opening an account, the customer is often lured into higher risk products that offer greater profitability to the broker and asset allocations are often ignored. In many cases, there is no effort to do any asset allocation and investors are heavily concentrated into equities or highly risky funds or structured products with commissions driving the decision.

In 2003, David Darst, Managing Director and Chief Investment Strategist for the individual investor business of Morgan Stanley, wrote The Act of Asset Allocation. On the fly leaf of the book is the following language:

> **Successful long-term investment performance is rarely a matter of luck or timing. Rather, it is a function of thoughtfully and prudently choosing a portfolio of investments for minimizing risk while maximizing return and strategically and tactically rebalancing assets to reflect changing markets,**

the creation of new asset classes and the global investment outlook.

Darst states in the forward of his book that, "Asset allocation is the most important factor in the performance equation of a multiasset portfolio." Various academic studies have agreed with Darst, concluding that over 90% of a portfolio's performance is due to asset allocation.

Morgan Stanley touts the same need for proper asset allocation and diversification in many of its advertising pieces. The following language appears in a marketing brochure for Morgan Stanley's personal portfolio[sm].

> **In the long-run, diversification and proper asset allocation are proven investment strategies that can help you achieve attractive levels of return while minimizing your overall risk.**

Morgan Stanley is not alone in touting the importance of proper asset allocation and diversification.

Many firms used to publish on their web-site and elsewhere, their model asset allocations at any given time. For example, the following table was compiled by Carnegie Partners as of January 5, 2000:

Wall Street Allocation Models	Stocks	Bonds	Cash
A.G. Edwards, Inc.	60	40	0
Bank America Robertson Stephens	80	20	0
Bear Stearns & Company	55	35	10
Credit Suisse First Boston	55	30	15
CIBC Oppenheimer	52	38	5
Donaldson Lufkin & Jenrette	80	15	5
Goldman Sachs & Company	70	27	0
J.P. Morgan & Company	50	25	25
Lehman Brothers, Inc.	80	20	0
Merrill Lynch & Company	40	55	5
Morgan Stanley Dean Witter	65	15	20
Paine Webber, Inc.	51	35	14
Prudential Securities	75	10	10
Salomon Smith Barney, Inc.	60	35	5
Warburg Dillon Read (UBS)	45	30	25
Wheat First Union	35	40	25
AVERAGES	*59*	*29*	*10*

The Wall Street Journal also periodically published similar information. This information is no longer readily available. It was likely discontinued because it became a tool to demonstrate how most firms failed to follow their own recommendations. The great disparity in these numbers also raised a serious question as to how so many high profile "experts" could have such major differences of opinion.

Customers deserve to know this information if it exists. The discrepancies between what was posted and what occurred in most accounts led virtually every firm to stop publishing this information. It is still worth asking a broker you are dealing with to share his firm's model asset allocation with you. These days, that will generally lead to interesting answers but seldom to any specific information.

Key Points:
➤ Make sure the asset allocations suggested by your broker meet your objectives.
➤ Ask for your broker dealer's model asset allocations.

***
HORROR STORY
The family, husband, wife and daughter, were originally from Arkansas. When the husband's business closed, the family moved to Dallas, where the husband went to work at a Target retail store. The wife took a job as a waitress and their daughter went to work as a clerk at a local bookstore. After a few years, the husband demanded a divorce and moved out-of-state. The wife received approximately $60,000 in the divorce settlement.

The wife was approached by a broker, a lady she had met at a charitable event sponsored by her church. The bulk of the wife's $60,000 was turned over to the broker to manage. The daughter was also encouraged to place her total savings with the broker "to earn more than the bank is paying." The daughter's funds, amounting to about $30,000, were moved from her local bank into the brokerage account. Immediately, the broker began an aggressive pattern of activity including the use of options. There was no asset allocation and no type of any organized planning. It was clear, in hindsight, that all decisions in both accounts were driven by what was good for the broker and not what was in the best interest of these modest investors.

The accounts were almost totally concentrated in a small number of highly volatile, high risk securities which were highly correlated. This amounted to having the investors put all of their eggs in one basket. In short order, the accounts were wiped out.
***

Making Inadequate Disclosures

A broker has a duty to disclose pertinent and appropriate information to an investor in order for that investor to make an informed decision. It is not enough for the broker to generalize that "everyone knows there is a risk in the markets and you could lose all of your money."

A broker owes his customer the negative duty "not to misrepresent" (misrepresentations), but also has an affirmative duty to use reasonable effort to disclose (failure to do so is an omission) to the customer any information which is relevant to affairs entrusted to him of which he has knowledge, information or notice. The broker is required to make known to his public customer all material facts within his knowledge which in any way impact the transaction or the subject matter of the relationship.

Together, misrepresentations and omissions form a claim for liability usually put forth by investors seeking to hold a broker dealer liable for the investor's losses based on reliance on what was said, or not said. Be demanding. Make sure you fully understand the risk of what you are being sold. If the broker can't explain the product or the risks in clear, easy to understand language, then you shouldn't be buying what they are selling.

A broker handling a customer's account has a duty to explain forthrightly the practical impact of the potential costs, fees and risks of the broker's recommended investments along with comparisons to similar or other investments.

Since the risks of making an investment will, under most circumstances, be a material fact, a broker who fails to disclose the detailed risks to the customer may be liable for material omissions.

When a broker makes a recommendation to a public customer concerning a particular security, the broker should have a clear understanding of the risks of that transaction. The broker is subject to a duty to recommend a security only after studying it sufficiently to become informed as to its nature, price and financial intricacies. A broker's duty to explain the risks has been described as an informational duty, the extent of which depends upon all the facts and circumstances. This includes the nature of the relationship between the broker and the customer, and the intelligence, experience and acceptable risk to the customer.

Investors are entitled to know the past performance history of a particular stock or mutual fund. Comparisons can be drawn between the risk of a particular investment and an appropriate "benchmark," such as the S&P 500, an Index or a comparable benchmark for other types of investments. Full disclosure in some instances might require the disclosure of beta, standard deviation or other commonly accepted measures of risks. Unfortunately, many brokers do not even understand the proper use of these valuable tools of risk measurement and are unable to fully disclose, much less explain, the risks. Sadly, many Wall Street sales trainers caution their salespeople (a/k/a investment advisors) to avoid "paralysis by analysis."

The customer has a right to know whether his registered representative is recommending a security based on the registered representative's own financial interest in the recommended investment rather than on the investment value of the recommended security:

> **"The duty of fair disclosure applies to the broker's commissions and other compensation where the nondisclosure may be material to the customer's decision to purchase the security the broker has recommended."** <u>NASD Enforcement v. Josephthal & Co., Inc.</u>, 2001 WL 1886873 (May 15, 2001).

Failure to provide a public customer with information about the costs, fees, expenses and restrictions on the individual investments, as well as commissions charged and trade costs, is damaging to public customers. Until this information is presented to public customers, they are at a disadvantage in any decision making on what to purchase.

Many of the shortcomings in this area represent a failure to supervise.

[61]

Dale Ledbetter, one of the authors of this book, has spent over 45 years in and around the securities industry. He has seen it all.

Prior to representing abused investors, he spent 33 years in the securities industry. During that time he worked as a salesman, compliance officer, branch manager and supervisory executive, he acquired first hand regulatory exposure when he was suspended for a failure to supervise.

Inadequate supervision is epidemic among many brokerage firms. Responsible parties have far too many duties which often leave too little time to properly supervise their employees. In truth, supervision is often intentionally lax because an employee's efforts are producing highly profitable results for the firm. The failure to supervise is often made a successful part of an investor's claim.

Don't assume that what the broker dealer tells you or sends to you is correct. Merrill Lynch recently agreed to pay a $3 Million fine for "supervisory lapses that led to overcharging its customers $32 Million." The firm also failed to send timely confirmations to over 230,000 customers on over 10½ million trades.

Had these acts been committed by a small broker dealer, FINRAs enforcement division would have likely shut them down. However, since a major Wall Street firm was the guilty party, they received FINRAs usual and customary "slap on the wrist."

Make sure you get all the information you are entitled to receive. Don't accept inadequate generalizations. Providing inadequate information and getting investors to "just trust" is one of the main tools brokers use to rip-off customers. There should be nothing left to the imagination. Rest assured, if a dispute later arises, the broker will likely claim that full and adequate disclosures were made.

Key Points:
- ➤ If the broker can't explain it in simple terms that you understand, then don't buy it.
- ➤ Don't assume that everything a broker tells you is correct. Get second opinions.

***

HORROR STORY
The Wall Street Journal recently reported that the clearinghouses of the Chicago Mercantile Exchange, the Chicago Board of Trade, the NYMEX and the COMEX, which make up the CME Group, have been deemed "too big to fail."

This designation was made by the Financial Oversight Council which, under the Dodd-Frank banking reform bill, is responsible for designating "systematically important" institutions, even those that are not banks or bank holding companies.

The Journal noted that the derivatives that are cleared through these entities are now positioned "...above the taxpayer safety net."

Interestingly, based on 2011 year end reports from banking institutions, J.P. Morgan Chase, Goldman Sachs, CitiGroup and Bank of America hold over $200 Trillion in notional value of these derivative products.

The government continues to provide protection for these risk taking institutions at the expense, and the ever growing potential expense, of American taxpayers.

The results of this "designation" haven't evolved into a horror story yet. It is a nightmare waiting to evolve and is a stark example of the power major banking institutions have over the U.S. government.

***

Encouraging Day Trading

There are really two types of active trading within a brokerage account. Both should be avoided by virtually <u>all</u> individual investors. The first is generally done by the client and is classified as day trading. Several discount brokers aggressively encourage day trading and offer a variety of "research" sources to support the activity. The ads virtually challenge the investor to prove their mettle, step up and reap the windfall profits just waiting to be plucked. The real motive is the outsized profits that the excessive trading generates for the broker.

The second type of active trading is done by the broker. This often evolves into churning in either a discretionary or non-discretionary account in which the client relies on the brokers supposed expertise. That "expertise" is usually fictional or wishful thinking. Don't fall for the commission generating kind of trading that rarely is successful for the customer. Investors should avoid day trading whether they are placing the trades or relying on the broker to make purchase and sale decisions and then executing those transactions.

Day traders try to time the market in an attempt to secure short-term profits in individual stocks. In the heyday of the tech boom there were stories galore of students, housewives and retired "day traders" who were making a bundle. Most of the stories were fictional. In fact, there were more losers than winners even in those heady days and most of the winners' stories were greatly exaggerated. Day trading for most is a fool's game fraught with high costs, great risks and little expectation of long-term success.

In the late 1990s there were numerous cases of abuse involving day trading. In an NASD Enforcement Proceeding, <u>Department of Enforcement v. Mazzei</u>, 1998 WK 176418 (June 24, 2008), the NASD found violations of NASD Conduct Rule 2310 based on the unsuitability of excessive trading recommendations.

The NASD found that broker failed to properly allocate the customer's assets, made aggressive use of margin, and engaged in day trading, which was a much more aggressive strategy than what was appropriate for the client. The NASD Hearing Panel noted that even if the customer wished to engage in speculative day trading, the broker was obliged to counsel them in a manner consistent with their financial situation.

Commission costs can be huge in a day trading account, even if the cost of an individual trade may be low. In the case discussed above, the customer would have had to earn 26% just to break even. That number represented a great deal for the broker, who made money whether the customer won or lost, but was hardly a good deal, by any reasonable standard, for the customer.

Brokers have an obligation to refrain from recommending such an unsuitable course for customers. Failure to do so will result in a viable cause of action against the broker. The NASD became so concerned about the widespread abuse of day trading that it adopted FINRA Rule 2270, which included a Day Trading Risk Disclosure Statement.

The Day Trading Risk Disclosure Statement requires that any FINRA member promoting a day trading strategy must post the Day Trading Risk Disclosure Statement on their website "in a clear and conspicuous manner." The language of the Day Trading Risk Disclosure Statement should serve as a sobering reminder and deter even the most egotistical of risk-takers from making foolish bets on their ability to beat the market:

> *Day trading can be extremely risky.* Day trading generally is not appropriate for someone of limited resources and limited investment or trading experience and low risk tolerance. You should be prepared to lose all of the funds that you use for day trading. In particular, you should not fund day-trading activities with retirement savings, student loans, second mortgages, emergency funds, funds set aside for purposes

> such as education or home ownership, or funds required to meet your living expenses. Further, certain evidence indicates that an investment of less than $50,000 will significantly impair the ability of a day trader to make profit. Of course, an investment of $50,000 or more will in no way guarantee success.

Many traders are so confident in their ability that they bypass full-service brokers, opting for low-cost firms and relying on newsletters, tips or exaggerated claims for information, leading to risky trading.

The Day Trading Risk Disclosure Statement continues:

> *Be cautious of claims of large profits from day trading.* You should be wary of advertisements or other statements that emphasize the potential for large profits in day trading. Day trading can also lead to large and immediate financial loses.

> *Day trading requires knowledge of securities markets.* Day trading requires in-depth knowledge of the securities markets and trading techniques and strategies. In attempting to profit through day trading, you must compete with professional, licensed traders employed by securities firms. You should have appropriate experience before engaging in day trading.

It is difficult to beat the market under any circumstances. It is virtually impossible when faced with the obstacle of trading costs associated with day trading.

Key Points:
➢ Don't day trade on your own.
➢ Don't let a broker day trade your account.

$$* * *$$

<u>HORROR STORY</u>
This story should be entitled, "You Lose Even When You Win."

The O'Briens had both worked hard, put their two kids through college and had accumulated a nice retirement nest egg in excess of $1.5 Million. A broker they met at their church heard they were retiring and sought them out offering "sound advice to assure a steady income in their retirement years."

The O'Briens liked the broker, were comfortable with his firm and agreed to allow him to handle their account. He assured them that he would put them in the "best income producing instruments he could find" that would also provide "safety first" for their irreplaceable funds. They placed strong reliance on the fact that his business card identified him as a *Senior Vice-President* of his firm.

He got them to sign all the necessary documents, assuring them that this was "just paperwork required by the government" and that they didn't need to worry about because "he had reviewed it."

The young broker proceeded to put over 90% of their account into a single fund that was loaded with the lowest tranches of complex structured finance products, many of which were collateralized by highly risky sub-prime loans. The funds were also leveraged, which greatly increased the risk. None of this information was given to the O'Briens who were assured the funds were "safe" and that the broker was watching them. The O'Briens left town to spend several months visiting their grandchildren.

It took only a small dip in the value of the collateral to wipe out the value of the funds sold to the O'Briens.

They returned from their trip and were told by the broker that their $1.5 Million was worth less than $150,000. Panicked, frightened and angry, the O'Briens sought legal help and soon filed a FINRA arbitration claim. Their case was heard before a three person panel and the O'Briens were given an award against the brokerage firm. The award for the O'Briens went into the FINRA computation as a <u>WIN</u> for investors.

However, a closer analysis of the numbers would prove the results were a long way from a victorious outcome for the O'Briens.

The total award, with no explanation as to how it was reached, was for $150,000. The claims for expert fees, hearing costs, attorney's fees and punitive damages were all denied. Adding insult to injury, the panel charged the O'Briens 50% of the hearing costs. The end results were as follows:

Award	$150,0000	
	-$50,000	Contingency Attorney's Fee
	-$5,000	Expert Testimony
	-$6,000	½ of Hearing Costs
	-$2,500	Miscellaneous Expenses
	-$63,000	Total Costs
Net Recovery	$87,000	

The original $1.5 Million deposited with the brokerage firm had become $87,000. The O'Briens sold their house, have both taken part-time jobs and have cancelled future plans to visit their grandchildren.

The broker lives in the same expensive home, drives a newer model of the same luxury car, and continues to golf three days a week at the nearby country club.

* * *

Using Titles to Mislead Customers

Would you trust a surgeon who never went to medical school to operate on you? Americans trust doctors (more than many other professionals) because society assumes that the medical profession has high standards. Presumably, anyone who becomes a medical doctor has climbed the ladder of a rigorous educational system including medical school and residency. Most take even more courses in order to specialize as surgeons, cardiologists, pediatricians, and more. Even then, they continue to attend conferences and educational programs to stay current with medical and technological advances.

Would you trust a pilot that never went to flight school? Just like doctors, pilots are another example of a profession that society assumes requires extreme, rigorous and specialized training. This often includes military service, flight school, thousands of hours of simulation and continued education in refresher courses. Now, let's shift to money. Who do you trust with your money?

Stockbrokers, investment bankers, financial analysts, financial advisors, financial planners and business bankers are all examples of the different types of known, or even unknown, titles and positions within companies in charge of your money. The million dollar question becomes:

> **Why aren't customers as diligent at knowing how qualified brokers are to handle their money as they are in relying on other experts and professionals?**

We are talking serious money here, such as your child's college fund, your retirement fund, your entire life's savings in the palm of people's hands who are, generally, little more than well trained salespeople. They are all too often trained to emphasize the positive aspects of the product they are selling rather than to understand and adequately explain the risks.

[69]

Of course, there are various licenses available to earn and "qualify" a person to be able to sell stocks and other securities to customers. However, the same rigorous and specialized training that goes into becoming a doctor, engineer or pilot is just not necessary to become an "investment advisor." If you are going to decide to invest with a particular "investment advisor" or financial company, make sure to get a complete profile of their educational background, qualifications, and licenses. Understand exactly what they had to do to get whatever titles are attached to their name. Get a profile on their work history. You are considering turning over your precious, hard-earned and, often, irreplaceable assets. This is a <u>MAJOR</u> decision. Treat it that way.

Enter into the process with realistic expectations. There are <u>no</u> historical precedents to indicate, regardless of what titles a broker or advisor may have, that they are able to evaluate products and select the right investments for their clients.

The broker should have their own investment history available as public information, similarly to how the SEC requires that the board of directors disclose their personal stock transactions in their own company. If an investor is ever forced to litigate, they find that the evidentiary discovery process subjects them to the equivalent of a "financial colonoscopy." In contrast, investors are unable, even in a FINRA arbitration, to get any significant information about the broker's investments or to discover if the broker was, in fact, doing the things he claimed to be doing.

Here's a challenge. Ask your stock broker to explain to you Nobel laureate Harry Markowitz's modern portfolio theory. See if they are able to explain it to you, the average person, in terms you are able to easily understand. If they are sufficiently trained and come from the proper background, this should not be difficult to explain. Remember, these people are commission driven salespeople. They have quotas to make, or they cannot earn a living. They are taught to scheme and plan with your money because, at the end of the day, the thrust of their limited training is to get the customer to buy something. They are not necessarily trained to do what is in the customer's best interest.

Many of the titles assigned by broker dealers to their employees are no more than a sham designed to trick customers into believing they really are dealing with a qualified financial "expert." The titles go way beyond generic monikers like "financial advisor." They often entail prestigious titles intended to portray an image of competence and general accomplishment. In truth, titles appearing on business cards, such as those on the following list, almost always attest to "production" or sales success and have little or nothing to do with proven results for customers or any type of industry expertise:

> Managing Director
> Executive Vice-President
> Senior Vice-President
> Vice-President
> Financial Planner
> Senior Analyst

Regulators neither approve nor regulate the use of such titles. There are scores of other loftier sounding industry titles that are used to impress and attract customers. As an interesting exercise, the next time you see such a title on a broker's business card ask them to explain what it takes for them to qualify for that title in their organization.

Customers who discover that their broker's designations or titles are obtained from a three (3) day course in a hotel often become emotional and angry. The designations are often part of a turnstile education with questionable content, testing and certification.

We often hear the sad lament from abused customers that, "I trusted him because he was a Vice-President."

In the April 2004 edition of *The Register*, the official publication of the International Association of Registered Financial Consultants, Inc. (IARFC), it is noted that the NASD was sufficiently concerned about the abuse of titles to issue the following caution:

> "Investors can sometimes become confused by the many designations used by investment professionals. You should be careful judging anyone's qualifications from a set of initials following a name. Use the selection box below to help you sort through the list of professional designations and to better understand what education and experience requirements are necessary for a designation and whether the granting organization mandates continuing education, offers a public disciplinary process, provides a means to check a professional's status, and otherwise ensures that a professional designation is more than just a string of letters."

Wall Street titles and designations are designed to aid the sales process. They are aggressively and effectively used to trick and deceive public customers.

Shocked? You should be. Be forewarned. Too many people have lost their life's savings and their futures as a result of being misled by brokers and the brokers' titles.

Key Points:
➢ Ask your broker what qualifications had to be met to earn the title appearing on his/her business card.
➢ Titles generally have no relationship to a broker's ability to select winning investments.

***

HORROR STORY

The broker was a close family friend of the investors. He persuaded them to move their accounts to his firm and directed all of the investments in the account.

One of the investments he selected was a private placement in which the broker had a personal ownership interest.

Over a period of several years, the broker actually confiscated additional funds from the account and also placed several of his other clients into the same private placement. Internal communications showed the firm was aware that the broker was selling interests in a private placement in which he had a proprietary interest. This information was never shared with the investor.

The firm's compliance procedures required written notification to be sent to the client whenever funds were deducted from the accounts. This was never done.

The firm denied any liability and faulted the investor for not taking adequate steps to protect their investment.

***

Having Investors Ratify Wrongdoing

Broker dealers defend liability claims by investors in almost every case by raising the "ratification" defense. They argue that unauthorized trades, churning, unsuitable securities and all manner of other conduct was "ratified," or "approved," by the investor, thus, eliminating any liability on the part of the broker.

Brokerage firms usually argue that the investor has ratified the conduct being questioned if confirmation slips and monthly account statements were received and not challenged. Of course, most investors don't know they've been ripped off until long after the point of original sale. Account statements seldom, if ever, reveal to an investor the specific nature or extent of wrongdoing. Ratification requires "informed consent:"

> **Ratification of unauthorized trading occurs only when it is clear from the circumstances that the customer intends to adopt the trade as his own with knowledge of the pertinent facts and the clear intent to approve the unauthorized action is**

[73]

> a precondition to ratification. <u>Syedle v. C.L. King &Assoc., Inc.</u>, Fed. Sec. L. Rep. (CCH) 97, 701 at 97, 261 (N.D.N.Y. May 23, 1993).

Meeting this precondition is difficult. For this reason, the ratification defense is rarely effective.

In addition, "the principle of ratification... does not apply to cases in which a customer's consent is obtained through misrepresentations." <u>Eichler v. SEC</u>, 757 F.2d 1066, 1070 (9th Cir. 1985).

The concept of "informed consent" has also been applied to cases involving unauthorized trading. In <u>Karlen v. Ray E. Friedman & Co.</u>, 688 F.2d 1193 (8th Cir. 1982), the court found that, with respect to a ratification defense, "the question is not simply whether [the customer] assented to the [unauthorized] trades; rather it is whether [the customer's] apparent assent was given voluntarily and intelligently with full knowledge of the fact."

A customer can't ratify a trade or course of conduct by doing nothing if the customer is unaware that the trade or conduct can, in fact, be rejected, reversed or rescinded.

Confirmation slips and monthly statements do not necessarily enable a customer to determine his overall position, or the total amount of real profit or loss occurring in the account, unless the customer is sufficiently skilled to elaborate upon them in order to make that determination. There can be no waiver unless the customer has knowledge of the right being waived.

Key Points:
> ➤ Open and read all mail from your brokerage firm.
> ➤ Protest in writing any unauthorized account activity.

Selling TIC Real Estate Investments

TIC stands for tenants-in-common exchanges in real estate investments in which two or more investors have an individual percentage interest in the real estate. In 2002, the IRS issued
[74]

regulations (IRS Rev.Proc. 2002-22) that allowed, under specific circumstances, TICs to be used in §1031 tax deferred exchanges. This ruling allowed investors to defer capital gains on their real estate property sales by exchanging the proceeds into TICs. The IRS regulations came at the time when the real estate bubble was getting underway.

Needless to say, Wall Street took immediate advantage of this opportunity in real estate to make huge fees. This led to the issuance by Wall Street of numerous private placements with questionable collateral for TIC offerings. Many of the offerings contained misleading and fraudulent information about the commercial real estate to be owned by the investors.

In NTM 05-18, it states that when TICs are offered and sold together with other arrangements, they generally would constitute investment contracts and, thus, securities under the federal securities laws. NTM 05-18 further stated that TIC interests are a type of non-conventional investment (NCI). In NTM 03-71, the NASD explained that members engaged in the sale of NCIs must insure that those products are offered and sold in a manner consistent with the member's general sales conduct obligations as well as address any special circumstances presented by the sale of a TIC investment.

Numerous investors were misled by Wall Street about the quality of the commercial real estate in the TIC investment. In addition, chances are that little or no due diligence was performed by Wall Street on the TIC investment. In the sales pitch, the broker often failed to disclose the specifics of the tenant(s) egregious lease terms such as, undisclosed fees and excessive fees to the sponsors and managers, conflicts of interest, and undisclosed financing arrangements affecting the real estate.

Wall Street designed the TICs for yield chasers. With aggressive sales techniques, the broker could persuade a prospective investor to buy into the TIC deal.

The sale of a qualifying real estate property is subject to a 15% capital gains tax rate. The sales load to Wall Street in these TIC deals averaged 7% to 10% or higher. The risk of owning a TIC for a few extra percentage points in yield is not enough spread to compensate the investor for swapping into an illiquid and risky product simply for tax deferral purposes.

Key Point:
> Do not allow your brokerage firm to **SELL** you TIC investments.

* * *

HORROR STORY
The best interest of the customer is not always the reason for a broker dealer's recommendation of a particular mutual fund. In 2004, the SEC, NASD and the New York Stock Exchange settled enforcement proceedings against Edward D. Jones & Co., L.P. (Edward Jones), a registered broker dealer. The settlement related to the firm's failure to adequately disclose revenue sharing payments that it received from a select group of mutual fund families. According to the Order issued by the SEC, Edward Jones entered into revenue sharing arrangements with seven mutual fund families, which Edward Jones designated as "Preferred Mutual Fund Families."

Edward Jones agreed to pay $75 Million to resolve the matter. That did not do much to help their customers, however. According to a Wall Street Journal article by Laura Johannes and John Hechinger, written in January 2005, Nancy Wessler, an 80 year old widow, was sold a mutual fund that caused her to lose 40% of her portfolio. What Wessler did not know was that her Edward Jones broker was induced to sell those particular funds through this revenue sharing practice known in the industry as "pay to play." Wessler had not been told that the advice to purchase the funds was clothed in incentives for Edward Jones. The practice of revenue sharing is not illegal if properly disclosed to customers, but Edward Jones neglected to properly disclose the extra benefits it was receiving for the sale of what Edward Jones termed "Preferred Funds."

According to SEC Press Release No. 2004-177, Linda Chatman Thomsen, Deputy Director of the SECs Division of Enforcement, said, "Edward Jones' undisclosed receipt of revenue sharing payments from a select group of mutual fund families created a conflict of interest. When customers purchase mutual funds, they should be told about the full nature and extent of any conflict of interest that may affect the transaction. Edward Jones failed to do that." In the same press release, Merri Jo Gillette, Regional Director of the SEC's Midwest Regional Office, added, "By not telling investors the whole story, Edward Jones violated the federal securities laws."

One class action suit filed by investors in the US District Court in Missouri, Case No. 4:04-CV-00086 HEA, claimed the revenue sharing agreement results were a significant factor in determining the size of brokers' bonuses. The claim stated that broker bonuses could add up to as much as $80,000 to $90,000 a year, and often averaged about a third of a broker's total compensation.

***

Chapter 3
How Wall Street Uses Mutual Funds to Rip Off Investors

All mutual fund investments are not bad. In fact, mutual funds may be the best way for many investors to go. However, long history tells us two important facts.

First, investors should choose passive funds that will reflect a market return rather than funds that are actively traded. Secondly, if an investor chooses actively managed funds, for whatever reason, they should seek out those funds with the lowest overall costs. Cost control should also be a major consideration even in the selection of passive funds.

Mutual funds are touted as practical alternatives to owning individual stocks, bonds or other investment vehicles. Investors are often told that money in mutual funds will allow them to put their financial concerns on autopilot. It doesn't often work out that way.

Before understanding the ways mutual funds can pose dangers, investors must first understand certain basics about mutual funds and about the mutual fund industry.

According to the 2012 Investor Company Fact Book[3], 44% of U.S. households own mutual funds. Sales of mutual funds to individual investors have increased substantially in the last 30 years. The following chart demonstrates the dramatic increase in retail sales of mutual funds in the United States.

---

[3]For more information from the 2012 Investor Company Fact Book 52nd Edition, See the website WWW.ICIFACTBOOK.ORG.

44 Percent of U.S. Households Owned Mutual Funds in 2011

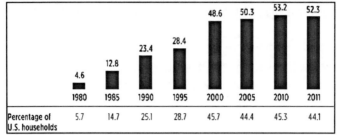

	1980	1985	1990	1995	2000	2005	2010	2011
	4.6	12.8	23.4	28.4	48.6	50.3	53.2	52.3
Percentage of U.S. households	5.7	14.7	25.1	28.7	45.7	44.4	45.3	44.1

Sources: Investment Company Institute and U.S. Census Bureau. See *ICI Research Perspective*, "Ownership of Mutual Funds, Shareholder Sentiment, and Use of the Internet, 2011."

Mutual funds accumulate money from many individual and institutional investors to buy and sell an array of assets such as stocks, bonds, real estate, precious metals and other assets. Mutual funds were originally designed to offer the individual investor asset diversification, liquidity, and professional money management with relatively low investment amounts. Mutual funds are operated by money managers who invest the fund's capital and attempt to produce capital gains and income for the fund's investors. Interestingly, mutual fund directors are generally selected by fund advisors rather than the Board of Directors selecting advisors.

Using the method of varied asset diversification, it is hoped that a loss on one holding will be made up by a gain on another. The holders of mutual fund shares gain the advantage of diversification to an extent that would ordinarily be beyond the means of an individual investor.

Mutual funds earn money for investors in several ways:

Net Asset Value (NAV): If the value of a mutual fund's portfolio increases (after deduction of expenses and liabilities), then the value (NAV) of the mutual fund shares increases.

Dividends and Interest: A stock mutual fund may earn income in the form of dividends. Bond mutual funds earn interest on the securities in its portfolio. The mutual fund will then pay shareholders the income (less expenses) it has earned.

Capital Gains: When a mutual fund sells a security that has increased in price, the mutual fund has a capital gain. At the end of the year, it is typical for a mutual fund to distribute these capital gains (minus any capital losses) to investors.

With respect to dividend payments and capital gain distributions, mutual funds usually provide investors with a choice. The mutual fund can deposit the payment in a cash account, send a payment in the form of a check, or the investor can have their dividends or distributions reinvested back into the fund to buy more shares (often without paying any additional fees).

Features of a Mutual Fund

Mutual funds, like all other investments, have advantages, disadvantages and risks. However, when it comes to mutual funds, there is such a lack of full disclosure that it is virtually impossible for an investor to accurately determine the advantage of one mutual fund over another. Whether any particular feature is an advantage for an investor will depend on the factors relating to the investor's needs. In evaluating mutual funds as an investment vehicle, it is important to also remember that a mutual fund is not guaranteed, nor is it insured by the FDIC. A mutual fund is not protected by any government agency. Even if the mutual fund was purchased through a retail broker inside a bank that provides FDIC insurance to bank customers, the bank still does not insure an investment in a mutual fund.

Broker dealers often sell mutual funds as an appropriate investment choice by stressing the following features:

Diversification: This is the attribute most often emphasized in selling mutual funds. The claim of diversification is that you "don't put all of your eggs in one basket." Mutual funds tell you that, since your investments are spread out over a wide range of companies and industry sectors, this can help lower the "risk" if a single company fails or a sector falters;

Affordability: Mutual funds, in many cases, help investors with limited resources make investments by offering relatively lower dollar amount requirements for initial purchases, subsequent monthly purchases, or both;

Liquidity: Investors normally redeem their shares at the current NAV (plus any unknown fees and charges assessed on redemption).

Professional Management: Normally, a money manager will research, select and monitor the performance of the securities the fund purchases. Sellers generally tout the manager's market timing and stock picking abilities.

Types of Mutual Funds

Mutual funds, whether passively or actively managed, will normally fall into one of three main categories: money market funds, bond funds (also called "fixed income" funds), and stock funds (also called "equity funds"). Each type of mutual fund has different features and different risks and rewards. Generally, the higher the potential return, the higher the risk of loss to the investor. A short description of each follows:

➢ **Money Market Funds**: A money market fund is a mutual fund that generally invests in low-risk securities. These funds pay dividends that generally reflect short-term interest rates. Unlike a deposit account at a bank, however, money market funds are not federally insured. Money market funds typically invest in government securities, certificates of deposit, commercial paper, or other highly liquid and low-risk securities.

Money market funds try to keep their net asset value (NAV), which represents the value of one share in a fund, at a stable $1.00 per share. However, the NAV may fall below $1.00 if the fund's investments perform poorly. Investor losses in money market funds have been rare, but they are possible.

➢ **Bond Funds:** A bond is effectively a loan an investor makes to the bond issuer. Issuers are sometimes the federal government (Treasury bonds) or a local government (municipal bonds), government-sponsored enterprises (GSE), corporations, (Corporate bonds) or sometimes foreign governments or international corporations.

The investor, or bond purchaser, generally receives regular interest payments on the loan until the bond matures, at which point, the issuer repays the principal to the purchaser. Bond funds pool money from many investors to buy individual bonds according to the fund's investment objective. Most bonds pay regular interest until the bond matures. Bond mutual funds are easier to buy and many pay monthly dividends compared to most individual bonds, which often have semiannual payments. Bond mutual funds also allow an investor to invest small regular monthly amounts and provide an easy asset to buy, sell, and trade on the open market. Bond mutual funds are usually a convenient investing approach for smaller investors.

Bond funds generally have higher risks than money market funds, largely because they typically pursue strategies aimed at producing higher yields. Unlike money market funds, the SEC rules do not restrict bond funds to high quality or short-term investments.

[83]

Since there are so many different types of bonds, bond funds can vary dramatically in their risks and rewards. Some of the risks associated with bond funds include:

<u>Credit Risk</u>	A bond issuer's ability to make all principal and interest payments in full and on time is a critical concern for investors. Most corporate and municipal bonds are evaluated for credit quality by Standard & Poor's, Moody's Investors Service and Fitch Ratings. Checking a bond's rating before buying is not only smart, but also simple. Bonds rated BBB or higher by Standard & Poor's and Fitch Ratings, and Baa or higher by Moody's, are widely considered "investment grade." This means the quality of the securities is high enough for a regulated institutional investor to purchase and own them.
<u>Prepayment Risk</u>	This is the chance that a bond will be paid off early. For example, if interest rates fall, a bond issuer may decide to pay off (or "retire") its debt and issue new bonds that pay a lower rate. When this happens, the fund may not be able to reinvest the proceeds in an investment with as high a return or yield.
<u>Interest Rate Risk</u>	This entails the risk that the market value of the bonds will go down when interest rates go up. Because of the inverse relationship to interest rates, investors can lose money in any bond fund, including those that invest only in insured bonds or U.S. Treasury Bonds. The longer the term of the bond, generally, the higher the interest rate risk will be.

Historically, bond funds have been less risky than stock funds. However, in recent years, the emergence of structured finance products has produced many bond funds that are comprised (at least in part) of highly risky and very complicated structured finance products, ultimately raising the level of risk dramatically in bond funds that contain structured finance products.
[84]

It may not be obvious to the average investor whether or not a bond mutual fund owns structured finance investments. Structured finance products can be extremely complicated, making it necessary to have additional information to determine whether or not a bond fund is appropriate. Beware of risky structured finance products disguised as bond funds.

> **Stock Mutual Funds**: The third type of mutual fund is a stock mutual fund. Simply stated, stock mutual funds (or "equity funds") are mutual funds that invest only in stocks. They are considered to be more risky than most other types of funds, such as bond funds or money market funds. Along with the greater risk, however, comes the potential for greater returns. Historically, when looked at over a period of many years, stocks have outperformed both bonds and cash investments. When stocks flourish, logically, stock mutual funds also prosper. Not all stock funds are alike, however. This type of fund can vary greatly according to stated objectives, management style, and the type of companies in which they invest.

> **Hybrid Funds**: A fourth type of fund worth mentioning is a hybrid fund that combines the features, risks, and rewards of two or more types of above-mentioned funds.

Costs of Mutual Funds

Actively managed mutual funds, for the purported advantages they may offer to the investor, can be very expensive. The costs incurred by mutual funds are passed on to investors and are seldom ever clearly and fully disclosed. Despite the fact that fees and expenses are an important consideration in selecting a particular mutual fund, it is extremely difficult, if not impossible, to evaluate the actual costs of a mutual fund. Because a mutual fund's performance is directly related to its total costs, investors are at a real disadvantage when trying to evaluate the merits of a mutual fund investment.

The SEC requires only partial disclosure of many mutual fund costs. Some mutual fund expenses are reported in documents that are readily accessible, such as the prospectus and marketing brochures. Some expenses are disclosed in a fund's Statement of Additional Information (SAI). This is a document that almost no investors, and very few investment professionals, are even aware of.

The Mutual Fund Expense Ratio

Part of the cost of owning a mutual fund can be found in the Expense Ratio. Investors are routinely informed about a mutual fund's expense ratio, either through the marketing materials or the first few pages of the fund's prospectus, as required by FINRA and the SEC. Investopedia.com defines the Expense Ratio as follows:

> **"A measure of what it costs an investment company to operate a mutual fund. An expense ratio is determined through an annual calculation, where a fund's operating expenses are divided by the average dollar value of its assets under management. Operating expenses are taken out of a fund's assets and lower the return to a fund's investors."**

The mutual fund expense ratio is expressed as a percentage of fund assets that are required to manage, advertise and administer the mutual fund. The management fee is used to pay the fund manager(s). This fee averages between .50% and 1.0% of the fund assets annually. Administrative costs keep the fund operating. These expenses include office overhead and marketing costs. Merrill Lynch or Morgan Stanley Smith Barney mutual fund expense ratios historically can run 1.5% to 2.0%. This number varies widely among funds.

What investors are rarely told about, however, are the sizeable expenses in addition to the costs included in the fund's expense ratio. These hidden costs, including trading costs and others, are paid directly from the pockets of individual investors and are very difficult to determine. Firms are very discreet in the ways in which they disclose, or attempt to hide, these costs. Investors are not aware of the many variable costs of operating a mutual fund, in part, because the SEC does not require mutual funds to disclose many of these costs as part of the expense ratio.

A brokerage commission is paid every time the fund manager buys or sells a security. Mutual fund brokerage fees are reported to the SEC in documents that are not easily accessed or understood by individual investors. Some of these expenses are usually disclosed in the SAI referred to above. However, unlike the prospectus, the SAI is not provided to an investor unless the investor requests it. Since most investors are not familiar with an SAI, it is rarely requested. As a result, few investors are aware of the brokerage commission and fees that are paid. They are equally unaware of other costs disclosed only in the SAI. The SAI is also a reservoir of numerous risk disclosures that distributors prefer not to call to the attention of investors.

To further hinder the investor's cost evaluation process, mutual fund "families" are allowed to group together the costs associated with all of the funds within the "family" when reporting trading costs. This makes it virtually impossible to track the trading costs of each fund separately. The best an investor can do is to average the "fund family" costs. The impact of investment costs cannot be emphasized enough. The SEC's website says:

> "Higher expense funds do not, on average, perform better than lower expense funds."

Russel Kinnel, director of mutual fund research at Morningstar concluded:

> "If there's anything in the whole world of mutual funds that you can take to the bank, it's that expense ratios help you make a better decision. In every single time period and data point tested, low-cost funds beat high-cost funds."

What these observations mean is that higher fees do not guarantee better returns. Sometimes you get what you pay for and there is value in paying a higher price. When it comes to mutual fund expenses, however, that is rarely the case.

A study done in 2005 by the Zero Alpha Group (ZAG) found that 43% of the real costs of investing in U.S. mutual funds were hidden from investors.[4] The ZAG study was conducted by Edward O'Neal, a PhD and then professor of Finance at the Wake Forest University Babcock Graduate School of Management, and Jason Karceski and Miles Livingston, both from the University of Florida.

The study reviewed 3,276 mutual funds. It found that mutual fund fees, including expense ratios and 12b-1 expenses, often seriously understate their "true costs" due to hidden costs that seriously undermine fund performance. The following quote from the study is astonishing:

> **"The study found that 43 percent of the funds' expenses were omitted from their expense ratios and that the transaction costs of some funds exceeded 400 percent of their expense ratios."**

The numbers were even higher when only considering small cap funds where the study found 46% of all small cap mutual funds had trading costs that were higher than the other annual fees investors pay. These "funding costs" impact investor returns and are among those costs that are rarely discussed with, or ever revealed to, investors.

---

[4] Jason Karceski, Miles Livingston, and Edward S. O'Neal. "Mutual Fund Brokerage Commissions." Working Paper, January 2004. (April 12, 2004).

The impact of costs can be seen in the examples shown below:

Investment Amount	Annual Return	Total Expenses	Total Expenses For 30 Year Period	30 Year Value
$100,000	2%	0.5%	$25,289	$155,847
$100,000	2%	1.0%	$47,150	$133,986
$100,000	2%	1.5%	$66,032	$115,104
$100,000	4%	0.5%	$45,283	$279,057
$100,000	4%	1.0%	$84,426	$239,914
$100,000	4%	1.5%	$118,235	$206,104
$100,000	6%	0.5%	$80,188	$494,161
$100,000	6%	1.0%	$149,503	$424,846
$100,000	6%	1.5%	$209,374	$364,975

NOTE: Total expenses include opportunity cost, which is the difference in return between a chosen investment and one that is necessarily passed up.

On an investment of $100,000 the costs have a meaningful impact. Given a 6% return, an investor paying 0.5% versus 1.5% has a 26.1% larger balance at the end of 30 years. Remember, expenses compound just like income. Warren Buffet has joined the clamor of those advising investors to be wary of fees:

> "If you have 2% a year of your funds being eaten up by fees you're going to have a hard time matching an index in my view."

Following are descriptions of many of the sometimes hidden mutual fund costs in addition to the disclosed costs included in the Expense Ratio. Investors need to be aware of these costs when considering the purchase of mutual funds, whether they be passive or actively managed funds.

***

HORROR STORY

The Martins had limited education and no previous investment experience. The husband, a construction worker, was injured in a work related accident and received a settlement of over $500,000. At the time, he and his wife were both in their early 30s and had three children under age 9. Mrs. Martin was trying to stay home and care for their children, especially since one of the kids suffered from a serious illness. The Martins had no idea about how the settlement money should be invested. Relying on an introduction from their neighbor, they met with a broker from a major Wall Street firm.

The Martins emphasized to their broker that the settlement money was to replace some of the income Mr. Martin would have earned in construction. Mr. Martin was training for a new career. The Martins knew that they would not be able to put any money aside for their children's education or for their retirement for many years since Mr. Martin was learning a new trade. It was absolutely necessary to preserve the settlement funds the family received. The Martins made it very clear to the broker that safety of principal was more important than growth.

The broker assured them their settlement proceeds would be placed in the kind of mutual funds that would offer protection of principal above all else. However, they were sold several mutual funds that invested in emerging markets and high risk technology companies. The broker sold them multiple mutual funds in small amounts that failed to meet break point qualifications for discounts. The broker sold the Martins products based on sales incentives for him, not what made sense for the Martins. Ultimately, the funds performed poorly relative to their peer groups and caused substantial losses. The funds were proprietary funds distributed by the broker's firm and were also very expensive to own. The fees and costs associated with the funds took huge bites out of any returns the Martins could have hoped for.

As a result of their trust in the broker, his firm's reputation, and due to faulty advice and lack of supervision on the part of the brokerage firm, the Martins ended up losing over $350,000.

[90]

The financial profile prepared by the firm stated that the Martins had a "moderate risk tolerance" although they expressly stated that the funds were to be saved for their children's college expenses and the Martins' eventual retirement.

About a year into the account relationship, the broker approached the Martins and asked for a loan in the amount of $10,000. The Martins were reluctant to refuse the loan because the broker was managing their accounts and felt that, since the broker was a Senior Vice President of his firm, he was in a position to do them financial harm if they refused to oblige the request for the loan. The Martins had no idea that this practice is strictly prohibited.

The Martins later found out that this was their broker's first job in the securities industry. They also learned that he was charged with failing to follow other customers' instructions, and with making unsuitable recommendations. It came to light that the broker was also borrowing funds from other customers.

***

Hidden Mutual Fund Costs and Strategies

Account Fee:

It has become a growing trend for investors to be charged a fee for "account maintenance" on accounts which fall below a set minimum.

Directed Brokerage Expense:

Wall Street firms often contract to sell the shares of a particular mutual fund companies' products. The brokerage firm, by providing access to its sales force, justifies higher commissions, which inflates the cost paid by the mutual fund.

Breakpoint Discount:

Investors can normally receive discounts for making larger purchases within a single fund or family of funds. Always ask about breakpoint discounts. Brokers will often advise splitting investments to prevent investors from reaching a breakpoint, thus assuring themselves of a larger commission.

"A" shares are shares with front end loads; "B" shares are no loads; and "C" shares usually have unique characteristics. The abuse is usually in the "B" shares when sold in quantities above the "A" breakpoints.

High Activity Trading Cost:

Many active stock mutual funds claim to have trading costs below 0.5%. However, many funds, especially small cap funds, have brokerage commission costs far above that number. Funds do not factor in the impact of these trades on share prices.

Also, while these percentages may seem relatively insignificant, they add up to real money. A recent study by Greenwich Associates found that trading costs of the average retail mutual fund was in excess of $16 Million per year. It is no easy task to determine the actual trading costs of most mutual funds. They are not part of the fund's prospectus and usually, even for partial information, investors have to go, as noted previously, to the fund's SAI. The SAI is described as "part of the prospectus" but is only provided to investors if a specific request is made.

Sales Load:

The sales load is the front end sales charge, or commission, paid by investors at the time they purchase shares in a fund. The front end load reduces the dollars used to purchase shares by the amount of the "load."

Deferred Load:

This is the load (sales charge) paid by investors when they sell shares back to the fund (redemptions). In a deferred load purchase, all of the purchase dollars are used to purchase shares so that more dollars are working for the investor immediately. Normally, the back end or deferred load is reduced over time depending on how long the investor holds the shares.

Many investors are led to believe that "no load" means no sales charge and are never told about the back end load.

Redemption Fee:

This is a "sales charge" under another name. It is a "charge" imposed on investors when they redeem shares. The SEC website describes it as follows:

> "Although a redemption fee is deducted from redemption proceeds just like a deferred sales load, it is not considered to be a sales load."

Clever disguise, but the result is a reduction of investment performance for shareholders.

12B-1 Fee:

These are the fees paid as trailing commissions to the brokers who sell the funds. They also include other advertising and promotional costs. This means that, as an investor, you are paying for the fund to sell itself to other investors.

Bid-Ask Spread:

Bonds almost always trade based on a bid-ask spread rather than on commissions. This deals with the difference between the lowest price at which a seller is willing to sell a security and the highest price a buyer is willing to pay. The difference between the bid and ask price is referred to as the spread. At any given moment, for example, a security may have a bid price of $99 and an asking price of $101. If a mutual fund buys a security for $102 and the mutual fund decides to later sell the security when the asking price is $104 and the spread has stayed the same, the fund will only receive $102. The spread thus cost the seller $2. Over time, spreads will have a significant impact on a fund that does a lot of trading, particularly in less-liquid holdings.

Exchange Fee:

Generally, exchanges of shares from one fund to another fund within the same family of funds involves no sales or exchange fee. However, some funds do charge an "exchange fee" for transfers even within the same family of funds.

Incubation Strategies:

The incubation strategy entails starting multiple funds simultaneously. The funds are operated for some period of years and the results are calculated. Those that do poorly are shut down with no public notice. The more successful fund produces performance information to Morningstar (which requires 3 years of performance) and gets a top rating.

This is similar to a strategy one broker shared with the authors. He said:

> "I tell half my clients the market is going up and the other half that it is going down. Then, after a short period, I divide all those in the 'up group' and tell half of them the market is going up and the other half that it is going down. Then, after the third time I've done this, the customers in that group think I am a genius and will do whatever I suggest forever!"

An extension of incubation strategies is "survivorship bias." This term is defined by investopedia.com as follows:

> "...tendency for mutual funds with poor performance to be dropped by mutual fund companies, generally because of poor results or low asset accumulation. This phenomenon which is widespread in the fund industry results in an overestimation of the past returns of mutual funds."

If ALL funds' performances were included, the results of the mutual fund industry would be decidedly less impressive than the numbers that are published. Also, it is much easier to predict a mutual fund's costs than it is to predict its performance. Using past cost data is a much more effective way to research the value of a potential investment as a fund's costs are much more likely to remain consistent than its performance.

Hidden Taxes:

Mutual funds do not pay taxes, but mutual fund investors do. Mutual funds must pay out income from the fund to investors. Proceeds from sales, dividends and trading actively all lead to taxes being owed by shareholders. Taxes are owed on dividends even if the dividends are reinvested. Individual taxpayers who purchase shares in December may be disadvantaged relative to an investor purchasing shares in January. This is rarely explained to investors.

Shelf Space Expense:

Mutual fund companies often contract with brokerage firms to offer "no transaction fees." However, the mutual fund company will often pay more marketing costs to the brokerage firm. This means there is no real savings for the unsuspecting investor.

Soft Dollar Cost:

The term "soft dollars" refers to the payments made to service providers. These costs vary from legitimate payments to outright bribes. These "in-kind" payments are supposedly made in lieu of cash (hard dollar) payments.

Mutual Fund Costs, Are They Worth It?

The following quote from Eugene Fama, Jr., from the University of Chicago, Booth School of Business, summarizes the impact of paying mutual fund costs:

> "After taking risk into account, do more managers than you'd see by chance outperform with persistence? Virtually every economist who studied this question answers with a resounding "no." Mike Jensen in the Sixties and Mark Carhart in the Nineties both conducted exhaustive studies of professional investors. They each conclude that in general a manager's fee, and not his skill, plays the biggest role in performance." [The higher the fee, the lower the performance]

Active vs. Passive Mutual Funds

Let's delve a bit more deeply into the active vs. passive fund argument. An actively managed fund is simply one where the manager attempts to beat market returns by picking investments, relying on market timing, actively trading or taking excessive risks in expectation of higher returns.

A passively managed fund, often called an index fund, simply tries to duplicate the performance of whatever index it follows by owning almost all of the holdings in the index.

The con game that active management can consistently beat passive market returns is not a recent phenomenon. The overwhelming evidence to the contrary is persuasive whether over a short period of a few years, or tracking back over a 30 year time frame.

ZAG, referred to previously, is made up of investment advisory firms with a commitment to passive investment strategies. Numerous studies by ZAG and others have supported the choice of passively over actively managed funds as it relates to costs.

Risk is a preference factor when comparing actively versus passively managed funds. William Sharpe, a Nobel laureate, created the Sharpe Ratio which Investopedia.com defines as follows:

> The Sharpe ratio tells us whether a portfolio's returns are due to smart investment decisions or a result of excess risk. This measurement is very useful because although one portfolio or fund can reap higher returns than its peers, it is only a good investment if those higher returns do not come with too much additional risk. The greater a portfolio's Sharpe ratio, the better its risk-adjusted performance has been. A negative Sharpe ratio indicates that a risk-less asset would perform better than the security being analyzed.

Not only do actively managed funds generally underperform the market, they generally do so while taking risks in excess of passive market exposure. Size is yet another factor supporting the selection of actively managed funds. According to the *2012 Investment Company Fact Book* (52nd Edition) "the average equity index fund had assets of $1.6 Billion compared to $374 Million for actively managed equity funds." Because the passive index funds are larger, they experience economics of scale which benefit investors. The growing movement by more investors shifting to index funds will only add to these economies of scale.

The holdings of many actively managed mutual funds are highly correlated, meaning that much of the protection afforded by diversification is lost or substantially reduced.

Gregory Baer and Gary Gensler wrote *The Great Mutual Fund Trap,* published in 2002. It is a highly educational book which addressed many of the pitfalls of active mutual fund investing. At the beginning of their book the authors share a revealing story as to why they wrote the book:

> Initially, the reason was frustration. While serving at the Treasury Department during the Clinton administration, we undertook a review of the investment performance of the Pension Benefit Guaranty Corporation. The PBGC is the federal government entity that stands behind the corporate pensions of millions of American workers. It had been investing in stocks – that is, hiring managers to beat the market, since 1976. The performance was remarkably poor. A dollar invested by PBGC in 1976 would have earned 44% by 2000 if it simply tracked the market. Moreover, the PBGC earned these below-market returns while investing in stocks that were more risky than those in the broad market.

Jeff Brown of TwinCities.com wrote an article titled, "Beating Index Funds Takes Rare Luck or Genius." In preparing the article, he asked Morningstar to look at the record of mutual funds over the

10 year period ending in October of 2004. The independent investment research firm determined that there were, at the time, 1,446 large-cap blend funds that invested in a similar asset class to the S&P 500. Over the observed time period, only 35 mutual funds matched or beat the performance of the S&P 500. That's only 2.4% or one in forty-one. Brown's sobering conclusion was:

> "if such a small percentage beat the index, many of them do it with luck, and there's no way to identify those that really are brilliantly managed...well that's why index fund investing is so attractive."

Another area where passive beats active funds is in the expense ratio. Below is a chart outlining the differences in mutual fund expense ratios in active vs. passive funds:

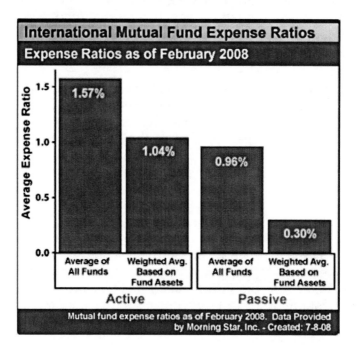

The average expense ratio on active funds is three times higher than its passively managed equivalent – and there is no clear justification for the increase in costs to the investor. The conclusion is simple and stark. Don't be sold actively managed mutual funds and remain highly cost conscious even in the selection of passively managed funds.

Key Points:
- ➤ Make cost consciousness the major factor in evaluating mutual funds.
- ➤ Invest in passively managed funds rather than actively managed funds.

***

HORROR STORY

Ms. Smith had lost her husband of 52 years just 24 months before the arbitration hearing. Ms. Smith brought the claim against a Wall Street brokerage firm because they sold her a single stock and then told her to hold the stock as it cratered and placed her in 2 separate variable rate annuities (VRAs) to replace the investments left for her by her late husband.

Ms. Smith was never advised or warned by the brokerage firm about the risk of over-concentration in a single stock or about the numerous risks of the VRAs she was sold.

The broker dealer also failed to advise Ms. Smith about each of the fees and expenses of the VRAs. The brokerage firm failed to disclose that they were paid a commission for selling her the VRA. In fact, she was told that there was no commission in the sale of the VRAs. No explanation was provided about the life insurance component which was extremely costly compared to the coverage provided. The fees were actually the least of Ms. Smith's concern. Within a few months the highly risky sub-accounts within her sub-accounts were down substantially.

Ms. Smith was told details about VRA expenses being way too high while having coffee with a friend, also a widow. The friend had also suffered losses in her VRA and when Ms. Smith began looking into the situation she was thwarted, misled, misguided and misdirected. After months of trying to get answers from the firm with no success, Ms. Smith hired an attorney to bring a claim in arbitration conducted by FINRA.

Ms. Smith ended up with three arbitrators, none of whom had ever ruled for an investor. One arbitrator had ruled five straight times for brokerage firms; one had ruled for the Respondent in both cases she had heard; the third arbitrator had actually ruled in favor of the Claimant but in that case the Claimant was a brokerage firm which was suing a former employee.

Despite protestations by Ms. Smith's counsel, FINRA approved the panel and the case went to hearing. In the case presented by Ms. Smith she requested damages of $350,000, which were her actual losses. She claimed both the stock and the VRAs she was sold were unsuitable for her, given her investment objectives and overall financial situation. Ms. Smith also requested assessment of all arbitrator fees, costs, expenses and attorney fees against the Respondent.

The result was a damage award of $7,500 to Ms. Smith. All other claims were dismissed and all other costs and expenses were ordered to be divided between the parties. The $7,500 award was not enough to cover her portion of the expenses as assessed. In the end, Ms. Smith paid approximately $3,500 to go to arbitration against a brokerage firm which stuck her with large holdings in a single, highly risky stock and two (2) variable rate annuities. Of course, given the $7,500 award, her case counted in FINRA's statistical system as a "WIN" for a Claimant.

*** * ***

Chapter 4

Misusing Annuities – The Good, the Bad and the Ugly

The very term "annuity" conjures up images of bountiful, safe investments. Investors are told their funds are safe, secure and guaranteed. The high costs, fees and often hidden risks are seldom fully explained or even adequately described. In some cases, this is intentional conduct bordering on fraud. At other times, it is negligent or even a result of the seller's own ignorance or lack of understanding.

So, what are annuities? Annuities are sometimes defined as mutual funds inside an "insurance wrapper." The insurance wrapper component provides for undefined, unknown and additional charges and for contract benefits which are purchased, and not found in mutual funds. Such added benefits include a death benefit, tax deferral, the right to certain payouts including payouts for life "annuitization" benefits, and other benefits.

There are fixed income annuities. There are defined or immediate payment annuities. There are also equity based annuities, variable rate annuities (VRAs) and equity indexed annuities (EIAs).

Banks raise funds by issuing certificates of deposit (CDs). Annuities are the fund raising tool used by insurance companies and compete with CDs for investor monies. Annuities are often sold as having the same primary characteristics as CDs when in fact, they are far more complex, costly and often far riskier.

Although securities industry rules prohibit stockbrokers or insurers from selling you annuities <u>that would be unsuitable for your situation, they often do it anyway because of the substantial commission attached to these products</u>. All companies have internal supervisory control systems to catch unsuitable annuity sales, but it rarely happens. Also, be aware that most states allow insurance salespeople, who do not hold securities licenses, to sell annuities products. This is done under the guise of the annuities being insurance products rather than securities.

The areas of greatest abuse have occurred in the sale of VRAs and EIAs. So let's explore those types of annuities and how Wall Street uses them to rip off investors.

Variable Rate Annuities – Troublesome at Their Best

The VRA product may sound good when presented by an aggressive Wall Street salesperson, but the costs, expenses, commissions and risks of VRAs make them an overly expensive and normally unsuitable investment for most investors.

VRAs are at best a complex, overly expensive, terribly unpredictable, risky, and generally misunderstood product. The lack of understanding is not limited to individual public customers, but to brokers, brokerage houses and experts who analyze these products. The complex nature of this insurance product sold by licensed securities sellers is **NOT** a good place to put your retirement savings.

Let's investigate further.

The sale of tax deferred annuities was, and still is, a popular way to defer paying taxes. Investors need to understand that some annuities are tax deferred products but, contrary to how they are sometimes represented, they are <u>NOT</u> tax avoidance vehicles.

While the premise of tax deferral to a later day is certainly attractive, VRAs are neither simple nor auto pilot products like a certificate of deposit or a savings account. Unfortunately, investors today are often sold a VRA with claims that it is as safe as a CD, which is simply not true. There is no FDIC or similar government safety net for these products. Millions of dollars worth of VRAs are sold every year into IRA and other tax deferred retirement accounts. Brokers often fail to disclose that investors are paying a hefty fee for an unnecessary and redundant feature.

The years since 2007 and 2008 have seen interest rates on savings accounts and for CDs as low as they have been in the entire lifetime of most investors. An investor who has made 6% on CDs in years past is hard pressed to sit by and watch a one year CD earn just 1% interest. The passing of time and the need to accumulate money for retirement makes the small return seem unbearable. However, losing principal is an even worse fate.

A VRA is a contract. As with any contract, investors are expected to read it and ask questions before signing it. As with any insurance contract, the purchasers rarely read or understand the contract before turning over their money to the seller. A VRA contract is not a simple document. It is an investment contract put together by insurance companies and sold to investors through brokers engaged in the sales of securities. Typically, the broker assures the prospect that the contract is "just a lot of legalese" and that they have already explained all the pertinent details.

Investors are drawn to the VRA investment idea, in part, based on the tax deferral feature. What they often fail to hear from the sellers of the VRA on the front end is that they are investing into the stock market through the VRA investment. Many investors who had been wiped out by the stock market and were looking to avoid risk, bought VRAs and got right back in the stock market and were again exposed to the very risks they sought to avoid.

In most VRAs, the insurance company provides the investor with a limited number of stock or bond choices in the form of "baskets" or "groups" of stocks and bonds chosen by the insurance company. The investor has no alternatives available for investment other than these baskets of securities or "funds" which are all given impressive names like "The XYZ Company High Yield Total Income Moderate Yield Fund." The names are rarely, if ever, indicative of the risks or costs of the named fund. By calling risk and expensive investments safe sounding names, the public customer is often misled.

VRAs are often compared to mutual funds, but this is a misleading comparison. Mutual funds have values that are capable of being tracked and presented with historical information on performance and costs. A mutual fund is, at least, more transparent than a VRA in the way that the stocks or bonds in the mutual fund are specifically identified. Comparatively speaking, a mutual fund provides more information and better information to a prospective investor than any VRA product. While the actual annual costs of a mutual fund may not be fully disclosed, the information is at least more complete and more easily ascertained than is true of a typical VRA. This type of information about any VRA investment is intentionally made more difficult to locate and determine.

FINRA Rule 2330 sets out the responsibilities of FINRA members regarding deferred VRAs. In summary, members can only recommend a VRA if it is deemed suitable and the customer has been informed, in general terms, of important features such as surrender charges, tax penalties, expenses, advisory fees, riders and market risk.

The broker's compliance with FINRA Rule 2330 must be documented and signed by the broker recommending the transaction.

FINRA has a long-standing history in noting the overall responsibilities of its members in the sale of VRAs. NASD NTM 99-35 provides an excellent summary of the product and FINRA's expectations from its members:

Background

A variable annuity is an insurance contract that is subject to regulation under state insurance and securities laws. Although variable annuities offer investment features similar in many respects to mutual funds, a typical variable annuity offers three basic features not commonly found in mutual funds: (1) tax-deferred treatment of earnings; (2) a death benefit; and (3) annuity payout options that can provide guaranteed income for life.

A customer's premium payments to purchase a variable annuity are allocated to underlying investment portfolios, often termed subaccounts. The variable annuity contract may also include a guaranteed fixed interest subaccount that is part of the general account of the insurer. The general account is composed of the assets of the insurance company issuing the contract. The value of the underlying subaccounts that are not guaranteed will fluctuate in response to market changes and other factors. Because the contract owners assume these investment risks, variable annuities are securities and generally must be registered under the Securities Act of 1933.

The underlying subaccounts that are not guaranteed are funded by a separate account of a life insurance company that, absent an exemption, is required to be registered as an investment company under the Investment Company Act of 1940. Variable annuities assess various fees including fees related, to insurance features, e.g., lifetime annuitization and the death benefit. The fees are typically deducted from customer assets in the separate account.

A distributor of variable annuity contracts to individuals is required to register as a broker/dealer under the Securities Exchange Act of 1934 and become a member of the NASD. The distribution of variable annuity contracts is subject to NASD rules.

Typically, variable annuities are designed to be long-term investments for retirement. Withdrawals before a customer reaches the age of 59½ are generally subject to a 10 percent penalty under the Internal Revenue Code. In addition, many variable annuities assess surrender charges for withdrawals within a specified time period after purchase.

Generally, variable annuities have two phases: the "accumulation" phase when customer contributions are allocated among the underlying investment options and earnings accumulate; and the "distribution" phase when the customer withdraws money, typically as a lump-sum or through various annuity payment options.

The myriad features of variable insurance products make the suitability analysis required under NASD rules particularly complex. NASD Regulation has addressed suitability issues in variable insurance products sales in *Notice to Members 96-86*. In that *Notice,* NASD Regulation stated that when recommending variable annuities or variable life insurance, the member and its registered representatives are required to make reasonable efforts to obtain information concerning the customer's financial and tax status, investment objectives, and such information used or considered reasonable in making recommendations to the customer. In addition, a recent NASD disciplinary action discussed members' responsibilities under Rule 2310 (Suitability Rule) as they apply to the sale of variable life insurance. (*See* In the Matter of DBCC No. 8 v. Miguel Angel Cruz.)

As described above, phase one of a VRA is the accumulation phase.

During the accumulation phase, an investor can make additional purchase payments, which can be allocated to the identified investment options. For example, 40% to a U.S. stock fund; and 20% to an international stock fund. The money allocated to each investment option will increase or decrease over time, depending on the fund's performance in relation to the overall movement of the stock market. In addition, VRAs often allow allocation of a part of the purchase payments to a fixed account. A fixed account pays a fixed rate of interest. The insurance company will reset this interest rate periodically, depending on prevailing interest rates.

The most important source of information about a VRA's investment options is the prospectus. VRA prospectuses almost never provide the investment options to an investor before the purchase of a VRA. It is, therefore, rarely possible to read the prospectus or discuss it with an accountant, or an attorney, before the investor purchases the VRA.

During the accumulation phase, the investor can typically transfer money from one of the identified investments to another without paying any income tax on investment income or gains, although there may be a charge by the insurance company for transfers. If an investor withdraws money from the VRA during the early years of the accumulation phase, they will have to pay surrender charges. In addition, they will have to pay a 10% federal tax penalty if they withdraw money before the age of 59½. Therefore, an investor has tied up money for years, or in the alternative, can be severely penalized for accessing their very own money.

At the beginning of the distribution phase, an investor may receive purchase payments plus investment income and gains (if any) as a lump-sum payment, or may choose to receive them as a stream of payments at regular intervals (generally monthly).

If the investor chooses to receive a stream of payments, they may have a number of choices on how long the payments will last. Under most VRA contracts, the investor may choose to have annuity payments last for a period of time that is set (such as 20 years) or for an indefinite period (such as a lifetime or the lifetime of a spouse or other beneficiary). During the distribution phase, the annuity contract may permit the investor to choose between receiving payments that are fixed in amount or payments that vary based on the performance of mutual fund investment options until it is exhausted.

The amount of each periodic payment will depend, in part, on the time period selected for receiving payments. Be aware that some annuities do not allow the withdrawal of money from an account once the investor has started receiving regular annuity payments. The terms of all VRAs must be reviewed to determine what limitations apply. By way of example, some annuity contracts are structured as immediate annuities, which means that there is no accumulation phase and you will start receiving annuity payments right after you purchase the annuity.

The VRA Death Benefit and Other Features

A common feature of VRAs is the death benefit. If you die, a person you select as a beneficiary (such as your spouse or child) will receive the greater of: (i) all the money in your account, or (ii) some guaranteed minimum (such as all purchase payments minus prior withdrawals).

By way of example, suppose an investor owns a VRA that offers a death benefit equal to the greater of the account value or total purchase payments, minus withdrawals. The investor has made purchase payments totaling $50,000. In addition, the investor has withdrawn $5,000 from the account. Because of the withdrawals and investment losses, assume the account value is $40,000. If the investor dies, his designated beneficiary will receive $45,000 (the $50,000 in purchase payments you put in minus $5,000 in withdrawals). The cost of death benefits in VRAs is rarely provided because the actual cost is often used to hide the commission paid to the seller.

VRAs may allow investors to pay a price for a "stepped-up" death benefit. Under this feature, the guaranteed minimum death benefit may be based on a greater amount than purchase payments minus withdrawals. For example, the guaranteed minimum death benefit may be the account value as of a specified date, which may or may not be greater than purchase payments minus withdrawals depending on how well the underlying investment options have performed. The purpose of a stepped-up death benefit is to "lock in" the investment performance and prevent a later decline in the value of the account. This feature carries a charge, however, which will reduce your account value, is usually never disclosed to the investor and is rarely worth the extra cost.

VRAs offer many other optional features, which also have extra charges to the investor. One feature, the guaranteed minimum income benefit, guarantees a particular minimum level of annuity payments, even if you do not have enough money in your account (perhaps because of investment losses) to support that level of payments. Other features may include long-term care insurance, which pays for home health care or nursing home care if you become seriously ill. All these features may sound appealing but are almost always more expensive than they are worthwhile.

VRA investors pay several different charges, most unidentified. Investors are rarely provided with information on the cost impact when they invest, because it would reduce an investor's willingness to purchase a VRA. These charges reduce the value of the principal amount invested in the VRA as well as the return on the investment. They include the following:

> **Surrender Charges:** Withdrawing money from a VRA within a certain period after the purchase, usually the first 8 to 10 years, will cause the assessment of a "surrender" charge, which is a type of sales charge. This charge may be used to pay the seller a commission for selling the VRA to you. The surrender charge is calculated as a percentage of the amount withdrawn, and the percentage declines gradually over a period of several years, known as the "surrender period." For example, a 9% charge might apply in the first year after a purchase payment, 8% in the second year, 7% in the third year, and so on until the surrender charge no longer applies. Some VRAs may allow the withdrawal of part of your account value each year without paying a surrender charge.

Mortality and Expense Risk Charge: The M&E expense is a certain percentage of a VRAs account value, typically in the range of 1.25% to 2% per year. The M&E charge compensates the insurance company seller for insurance risks it assumes under the contract. Profit from the M&E risk charge is used to pay the insurer's costs of selling the VRA.

Administrative Fees: This represents charges to cover record-keeping and other administrative expenses for VRAs. The fees are charged as a flat annual account maintenance fee or as a percentage of the account value (usually around 0.15% per year). Again, these costs are rarely discussed or divulged to investors.

Underlying Fund Expenses: Investors will also indirectly pay the fees and expenses imposed by the funds that are the underlying investment options for your VRA. The investor, once again, is rarely provided with this information.

Fees and Charges for Other Features: Special features offered by some VRAs, such as a stepped-up death benefit, a guaranteed minimum income benefit, or long-term care insurance, often carry additional fees and charges. The costs for these features often exceed the value to the investor by large amounts.

Other charges, such as initial sales loads, or fees for transferring part of the investor's account from one investment option to another, may also apply. Investors are rarely given time to understand or discuss these options.

Given all we have said about VRAs, how can one explain the continuing volume of sales? As mentioned, VRAs actually have disadvantages, are usually illiquid for up to ten (10) years, have trivial and often valueless life insurance components, and yet sales have continued. The truth is that VRAs are the classic example of a

[110]

product which is <u>SOLD</u> to investors because they pay large commissions. Brokers, like any other commissioned salesperson, must sell products to make a living. There are few, if any products, which match VRAs in having the guarantee of a fat upfront commission along with some trailing commissions.

FINRA often cites its efforts to educate investors as one way it offers "investor protection." Unfortunately, the vast majority of FINRA educational materials and warnings go to FINRA members <u>NOT</u> to investors. The average person is not aware that FINRA exists. They would not know how to access the FINRA educational material, especially on complex products like VRAs.

FINRA has made a regular stream of communications <u>TO ITS MEMBERS</u> through *Notices to Members* (NTMs) regarding VRAs:

NTM 07-36
> ...it is incumbent upon firms to educate their prospective representatives in understanding that a change of employment is not by itself a suitable basis for recommending a switch from one product to another and to supervise with respect to such conduct.

<u>Lesson to investors</u>: Question the reason for changing from one VRA product to another. The exchange is costly and is normally for the broker's benefit, not the customer's.

NTM 07-53
> Deferred variable annuities are hybrid investments containing both securities and insurance features. They offer choices among a number of complex contract options, which can cause confusion for both the individuals who sell them and customers who buy them. FINRA developed Rule 2821 to enhance broker-dealers' compliance and supervisory systems and provide more comprehensive and targeted protection to investors regarding deferred variable annuities.

Lesson to investors: These are highly complex products which require close compliance and supervision of the sellers. Beware of owning such a product.

> NTM 08-39
> D. <u>Guarantee Claims and Riders</u>
> Communications concerning variable insurance products frequently emphasize guarantees or riders, particularly to the extent that they protect an investor in a down market. FINRA recognizes the need to communicate the features of these guarantees and riders through sales material. However, it is equally important that these communications discuss guarantees and riders in a fair and balanced manner.

Lesson to investors: You are often told the "good" about VRAs but are seldom told the "bad and the ugly."

> NTM 09-32
> FINRA Rule 2821 Members' Responsibilities Regarding Deferred Variable Annuities
> (e) Training Members shall develop and document specific training policies or programs reasonably designed to ensure that associated persons who effect and registered principals who review transactions in deferred variable annuities comply with the requirements of this Rule and that they understand the material features of deferred variable annuities, including those described in [sub]paragraph (b)(I)(A)(i) of this Rule.

Lesson to investors: Despite this requirement, there is a shocking lack of knowledge on the part of those who sell VRAs. Many others, who do fully understand the risks, as well as the rewards, fail to properly communicate that information.

> FINRA News Release 2/15/07
> FINRA fines Fifth Third Securities $1.75 Million for 250 Unsuitable Variable Annuities Transactions.

[112]

<u>Lesson to investors</u>: Be wary of bank affiliated broker dealers. Investors often tend to give credibility to the promises of a broker dealer because of a bank affiliation. That confidence has proved to be misplaced on many occasions.

> **FINRA News Release 1/29/08**
> **FINRA Fines Banc One For Unsuitable Variable Annuity Sales, Inadequate Supervision of Fixed-to-Variable Annuity Exchanges.**

<u>Lesson to investors</u>: Another example of abuse by a bank affiliated broker dealer. In this case, 21 of the 23 investors were over 70 years old.

This stream of information from FINRA is valuable for investors and might save many of them from falling into the burning pit of VRAs. Alas, it is, for the most part, like a tree falling in the forest which makes no sound because there is no one there to hear it.

Investors are now being aggressively lured by the "bonus credit" features of some VRAs. The "bonus" adds to the contract value based on a specific percentage, usually 1% to 5% of the purchase payments.

If the customer purchases a VRA contract that offers a bonus credit of 3% on each purchase payment and the investor makes a purchase payment of $20,000, the insurance company issuing the contract adds a bonus of $600 to the investor's account.

There is a trade off, of course, but not favoring the investor. Frequently, insurers will charge for this fabricated bonus credit in one or more of the following ways:

> ➤ <u>Higher Surrender Charges</u>: Surrender charges may be higher for a variable annuity that pays you a bonus credit than for a similar contract with no bonus credit.

[113]

➢ <u>Longer Surrender Periods</u>: Your purchase payments may be subject to surrender charges for a longer period of time than they would be under a similar contract with no bonus credit.

➢ <u>Higher Mortality and Expense Risk Charges and Other Charges</u>: Higher annual mortality and expense risk charges may be deducted for a variable annuity that pays you a bonus credit. Although the difference may seem small, over time it can add up. In addition, some contracts may impose a separate fee specifically to pay for the bonus credit.

Before purchasing a VRA with a bonus credit, ask yourself — and the financial professional who is trying to sell you the contract — whether the bonus credit is worth more to you than any increased charges you will pay for the bonus. This might depend on a variety of factors, including the amount of the bonus credit and the increased charges, how long an investor holds their annuity contract, and the return on the underlying investments. You also need to consider the other features of the VRA to determine whether it is a good investment for you, which 99.9% of the time, it is not.

Investors should also note that a bonus may only apply to their initial premium payment, or to premium payments they make within the first year of the VRA contract. Further, under some VRA contracts, the insurer will take back all bonus payments made to you within the prior year or some other specified period <u>if you make a withdrawal, if a death benefit is paid to your beneficiaries</u> upon your death, or in other circumstances. There are usually few investors who can follow these misdirection plays by the Seller. It is all, by design, to confuse investors while the broker says "just sign here!"

Renowned author Steven Covey advises readers to "Begin With the End in Mind." Investors can learn, much about VRAs by analyzing past reinforcement actions. For example:

> *NASD Enforcement* v. *Josephthal & Co., Inc.,* 2001 WL 1886873 (May 15, 2001). Brokers owe a fundamental duty of fair dealing to their customers. Embedded in this duty is the requirement that when making a recommendation, the broker must disclose facts bearing on the risks associated with the recommended security that he knows and that are reasonably ascertainable. Conversely, [w]here the [broker] lacks essential information about a security, he should disclose this as well as the risks which arise from his lack of information. This duty of fair disclosure applies to the broker's commissions and other compensation where the non-disclosure may be material to the customer's decision to purchase the security the broker has recommended.
>
> The failure to disclose such commissions deprives the customer of the knowledge that his registered representative might be recommending a security based upon the registered representative's own financial interest rather than the investment value of the recommended security. Misrepresenting or omitting to disclose a broker's financial or economic incentive in connection with a stock recommendation constitutes a violation of the antifraud provisions.
>
> Brokers are not excused from the duty to disclose such commissions and compensation by the fact that there is not a specific rule requiring the disclosure of non-excessive sales credits. Cf. *SEC v. Feminella,* 947 F. Supp. 722, 731 (S.D.N.Y. 1996) (failure to disclose sales credit added to markup violated the antifraud provisions of the federal securities laws). Indeed, "the SEC has established through its enforcement actions the

principle that charging undisclosed excessive commissions constitutes fraud." *See Ettinger v. Merrill Lynch, Pierce, Fenner & Smith,* 835 F.2d 1031, 1033 (3d Cir. 1987).

Virtually all claims in VRA cases relate to the seller's failure to disclose the true nature and full extent of the risks involved in investing in VRAs. Shockingly, we find these failures to disclose occur in the vast majority of VRA sales, especially when made to elderly retirees.

According to the Insured Retirement Institute (IRI) variable rate annuity sales in 2011 were up 28% from 2010, topping $27.7 Billion. This represented, according to Morningstar, the strongest year for VRA sales since 2007.

We have devoted a great deal of space to VRAs. The reason for that concentration is that this product is increasingly being used by broker dealers to generate large commissions at the expense of trusting investors. A lot of what we have discussed is complicated. The advice is simple: Don't buy variable rate annuities.

***

HORROR STORY

Reverend White and his wife Martha lived off limited income and devoted their time and energy to serving the members of their congregation. The Whites had documented income of less than $50,000 per year and a net worth of less than $50,000. In opening a small brokerage account, the Whites made it clear that they were more concerned with preservation of capital than growth. Despite their wishes, the brokerage firm listed their risk tolerance as moderate to aggressive and growth as their investment objective. The funds the Whites turned over to the Wall Street brokerage firm came from an inheritance. It was made clear to the brokerage firm that these were irreplaceable funds which came from a one-time event.

The Whites opened a discretionary fund giving the broker complete authority to manage their account. They made it clear that they knew nothing about securities and were totally relying on the broker and the expertise available to her within her firm.

In response to the broker's inquiry about insurance, they made clear that they had an adequate policy through the church and did not want to pay for any product which included additional insurance coverage. Despite their request, 100% of the irreplaceable funds were placed into a variable rate annuity.

The holdings within the annuity sold to the Whites were heavily concentrated in highly risky and volatile tech stocks, ultimately causing the Whites to lose over 90% of their investment.

The brokerage firm denied any liability, claiming that all the losses were attributable to market declines. In fact, during the time the Whites were suffering devastating losses, the S&P was down only 22%, the Lehman bond index made gains, and the Dow Jones lost 6%.

Clearly the Whites were sold a product which was not suitable given their financial status and investment objectives. Ultimately, after filing an arbitration claim, the brokerage firm, while denying the Whites had been victimized, did agree to a substantial settlement with the Whites.

***

Equity Indexed Annuity

An Equity Indexed Annuity (EIA) is a fixed annuity that offers a guaranteed interest rate during the accumulation phase. As with other annuities, an EIA contains provisions that guarantee the insurance company will pay a minimum interest rate. However, unlike a standard fixed annuity, the interest rate is not at a fixed rate set by the insurance company. Instead, it is connected to the movement of the particular underlying index to which the annuity is tied, such as the Dow Jones Industrial Average or the S&P 500. If investors could receive the full benefits of upturns in the stock market without the risk of downturns, it would be the ideal investment, but EIAs provide no such returns.

Investors in an EIA do not get the full benefit of increases in the value of the underlying index. The fine print in an EIA contract normally contains provisions that set the participation rate and specifies how much of an increase the investor is entitled to receive. The insurance company fees are also deducted before EIA owners receive payments. These fees are substantial.

If the participation rate is 80% and the index increases by 9%, the investor is credited with a gain of only 7.2%, which is .80 times 9. If you read the participation rate in an EIA, you will also find that you may wish to keep reading after you have gotten to that paragraph, because in some EIAs, the insurance company only guarantees a participation rate for a single year. Others may lock in the participation rate for the entire period, but that is becoming less and less the norm.

A large part of the investment return of stock indexes involves stock dividends. However, in an EIA there are often provisions which state that dividends are not considered in determining the payment to investors.

In short, investors should realize and are often not told that they are receiving only a portion of the index performance and are not receiving any part of the dividend payments.

There is another limitation to investor returns in an EIA. In the fine print of an EIA is an "interest rate cap." EIAs normally have an interest rate cap limiting what the insurance company will pay regardless of increases in the underlying index. For example, if the interest rate cap is 10%, that is the top rate you will receive regardless of the fact that the underlying stock index may go up 20% or more during a given year.

EIAs also have heavy administration fees, usually running to 3% or more. If the index goes up by 8%, the actual return credited to investors is only 5%. The fee may be assessed in lieu of participation rate provisions. However, some insurance companies have EIAs that <u>charge both fees</u>. Remember, not all EIAs are created equally.

Before investing in an EIA, make sure to read from cover to cover all materials relating to this investment. If you have already purchased the EIA and were not given the opportunity to read the materials, you should immediately do so now to determine whether or not you have been hoodwinked. You should make sure, after reading the materials, that you understand all fees and costs, actual, potential and mathematically possible.

It is a simple concept to overlook, but whether or not your EIA pays you simple or compound interest can have a significant impact on your return. If your EIA pays simple interest only, you have yet another limiting factor in your return.

If an investor cashes in all or a portion of the EIA before the term of the annuity is up, before the accumulation period is completed or before the distribution period is completed, they will be subject to strict financial penalties. This is a harsh penalty designed to prevent investors from having access to their own money. Fortunately, the withdrawal charge may go down or even be eliminated during the latter years of the annuity. This will vary with each company and with the EIAs the company offers.

<u>Key Points:</u>
➤ The fees, costs and risks of variable rate annuities and equity indexed annuities outweigh the benefits.
➤ Do not be deceived by misleading advertising used to tout these high cost products.

***

<u>HORROR STORY</u>

Murray was, by any reasonable measure, a totally unsophisticated investor. He spent his entire career working at a manufacturing plant in the Midwest. He had no investment courses or training of any kind in his educational history. This total lack of meaningful investment experience and limited education caused him to accept, without question, whatever the broker dealer purchased for him in his account.

Murray was born in 1940 and spent his entire career as a laborer at an assembly plant. He has been married for 41 years to his wife. The couple has two grown children. In 2007, Murray retired after building a retirement fund worth over $250,000. Rather than take the monthly payments for life as set up in the company plan, Murray was persuaded to invest his retirement fund by a broker who made a presentation to company employees. Murray and his wife had known the broker since he was a child because Murray's father was President of the local union and the broker's father was also a union member. The broker assured Murray that he could get more income than offered by the company pension plan by investing in a VRA. Murray followed the advice of his trusted investment advisor and turned over his entire retirement account to the broker who invested it in a VRA from Jackson National Life.

The broker set up monthly income payments for Murray that included only what was necessary for basic living expenses and taxes. Without consulting with Murray, he also sold him a "rider" that allowed for 20% in additional withdrawals, called a "Free Withdrawal Benefit Endorsement" beyond what the VRA would otherwise allow.

Murray made regular monthly withdrawals in accordance with the original plan established. He was told that the approximate $2,000 per month withdrawals for living expenses were going to last the rest of his life. He was assured there would be a death benefit as well.

On multiple occasions, Murray asked the broker if he could really afford the monthly payments. The broker confirmed to him that the annuity was easily making enough money to pay for the money he was using for living expenses.

In January 2011, however, Murray received the last of his withdrawals. This came as a complete shock to Murray and his wife. He was told that he had no value left in his account and that there was no longer even a death benefit.

Through losses in the underlying securities within the VRA, Murray's account was abolished in just a few short years. The withdrawals Murray made were not made from the income of the annuity, but from his own principal, which was ever decreasing as the markets declined. Murray has major health issues and is no longer able to work. His wife now works part time as a housekeeper to supplement the small amount of social security the couple receives.

* * *

Section 2

Structured Finance

***
HORROR STORY

The New York Times
nytimes.com

The Debt Crisis, Where It's Least Expected
By GRETCHEN MORGENSON
Published: December 30, 2007

THE Indiana Children's Wish Fund, which grants wishes to children and teenagers with life-threatening illnesses, got an early Christmas gift nine days ago. Morgan Keegan, a brokerage firm in Memphis, made an undisclosed payment to the charity to settle an arbitration claim; the Wish Fund said it had lost $48,000 in a mutual fund from Morgan Keegan that had invested heavily in dicey mortgage securities.

Coming less than two months after the charity filed its claim, and as a reporter was inquiring about its status, the settlement is a rare consolation for an investor amid all the pain still being generated by the turmoil in the once-bustling mortgage securities market. Before the Wish Fund reached its settlement, its mortgage-related losses meant that nine children's wishes would go ungranted.

Against the backdrop of all the gigantic numbers defining the subprime debacle, the Wish Fund's losses look like small potatoes. The crisis has generated almost $100 Billion in losses or write-offs at the world's largest financial institutions, cost a couple of Fortune 100 chief executives their jobs, wiped out billions of dollars in stock market value and hammered the reputations of the nation's top credit rating agencies. Reports of the devastation that foreclosures are wreaking on borrowers also bring home the effects of this remarkable financial mess.

Still, the Wish Fund's experience is instructive because so little has emerged about the losses that investors have incurred in these securities, perhaps because few holders have wanted to disclose them. Some investors may still not know how much they have been hurt by the crisis.

As this debacle unfolds, accounts of investor losses in mortgage securities will come to light. And Wall Street's role as the great enabler — providing capital to aggressive lenders and then selling the questionable securities to investors — will be front and center.

Richard Culley, a blind lawyer in Indianapolis, founded the Wish Fund in 1984; since then, it has granted 1,800 wishes to children ages 3 to 18. The fund has roughly $1 Million in assets and is not affiliated with the national Make-A-Wish Foundation. Local medical centers submit names for potential recipients.

The Wish Fund's foray into mortgage securities began in June, when Terry Ceaser-Hudson, the executive director, consulted her local banker, Steve Perius, about certificates of deposit coming due in the charity's account. She said the banker, with whom she had done business for 20 years, suggested that she invest the money in a bond fund offered by Morgan Keegan. The firm is an affiliate of her banker's employer, Regions Bank.

Ms. Ceaser-Hudson's banker put her in contact with a Morgan Keegan broker to help her make a decision. Mr. Perius did not return a phone call seeking comment.

"I thought I was making a lateral move from the C.D.'s into this fund," Ms. Ceaser-Hudson said. "The broker said he'd put some thought into this and he had something perfect for the Wish Fund that was extremely safe."

That broker was Christopher Herrmann, and when Ms. Ceaser-Hudson met him at her banker's office, she quizzed him about the risks in the Regions Morgan Keegan Select Intermediate Bond fund, which he recommended.

"The first thing I said to him when I sat down was, 'I want to make sure that I understand this: you're telling me that this is as safe as a money market or C.D., because we cannot afford to lose one single penny,'" she recalled. "He said, 'This has been good for years,' so I thought, 'O.K.'"

On June 26, the Wish Fund put almost $223,000 into the Morgan Keegan fund. The charity's timing could not have been worse. That same week, two Bear Stearns hedge funds, with heavy exposure to mortgages, were collapsing. Turmoil in the mortgage market, which had been percolating since late winter, was about to explode.

AT the helm of the Morgan Keegan fund was James C. Kelsoe Jr., a money manager at the brokerage firm's asset management unit, based in Birmingham, Ala. A longtime bull on mortgage securities, Mr. Kelsoe rode that wave and earned a reputation as a hotshot money manager. As of June 30, he also oversaw six other Morgan Keegan bond funds, which included about $4.5 Billion in assets.

One of Mr. Kelsoe's major suppliers of mortgage securities was John Devaney, 37, a flashy mortgage trader and founder of United Capital Markets, a brokerage firm in Key Biscayne, Fla. During the mortgage boom, Mr. Devaney built up a net worth of $250 Million, he told The New York Times in an interview early this year.

However much both men initially prospered from doing business together, some investors who wound up holding Morgan Keegan's mortgage securities were less fortunate — the Wish Fund, for example.

More than two weeks after Ms. Ceaser-Hudson invested in the Morgan Keegan fund, she received her first brokerage statement. She said she was stunned to learn that within days of its initial investment in the bond portfolio, the Wish Fund had lost $5,000. By late September, with the credit markets frozen and the net asset value of the bond fund plummeting, Ms. Ceaser-Hudson ordered the stake to be sold. She received about $174,000, representing a loss of 22 percent within 90 days.

On Nov. 2, she filed an arbitration case against Morgan Keegan, contending that Mr. Herrmann's investment recommendation was unsuitable for the Wish Fund and that he had breached his duty to it. A spokeswoman for Morgan Keegan said that neither Mr. Kelsoe nor Mr. Herrmann would comment for this article. "Jim Kelsoe is fully focused on managing his fund portfolios during these volatile market conditions," said the spokeswoman, Kathy Ridley.

The Morgan Keegan fund, which had assets of about $1 Billion in March, is down almost 50 percent this year. It was weighted with risky and illiquid mortgage-related securities.

For example, at the end of September, the intermediate fund in which Ms. Ceaser-Hudson invested had almost 17 percent of its assets in mortgage-related securities — including collateralized mortgage obligations, home equity loans and pools of mortgages that were again combined into collateralized debt obligations. Mortgage exposure in the six other portfolios that Mr. Kelsoe manages ranged recently from 5 percent to 14 percent.

For several years, Mr. Kelsoe's embrace of mortgage securities paid off for his clients. His fund was started in March 1999 and generated positive returns each year until 2007. Through the end of 2006, it had an average annual return of about 4.5 percent, after taxes.

Mr. Kelsoe's love affair with mortgage debt paralleled that of Mr. Devaney, one of those colorful and cocky Wall Street figures who appear during market booms only to sink from sight in the ensuing busts.

Living in a home on the Intracoastal Waterway, Mr. Devaney surrounded himself and his family with Renoirs and Cézannes. Outside floated his 142-foot yacht called Positive Carry, a reference to borrowing money at a lower rate than you receive on your investment. He also owned the house that was used as the setting for the Al Pacino film "Scarface."

In addition to running United Capital, Mr. Devaney also oversaw United Real Estate Ventures and several hedge funds with roughly $650 Million under management as of early this summer. In July, he halted redemptions in the hedge funds as the market swooned for his favorite mortgage securities.

A 2004 profile of Mr. Devaney in US Credit magazine said that he considered Mr. Kelsoe one of his most valued customers. United Capital Markets, the article said, was most often a buyer of bonds from Wall Street and mortgage issuers; the firm had far fewer clients to whom it sold those securities. One of the biggest buyers was Mr. Kelsoe and his mutual funds.

"I have found John to be very aggressive in his ability to find interesting trading ideas," Mr. Kelsoe was quoted as saying of Mr. Devaney in the profile.

Mr. Devaney did not return a phone call seeking comment.

Thomas A. Hargett, a lawyer at Maddox Hargett & Caruso in Indianapolis, represented the Wish Fund in its arbitration claim against Morgan Keegan. He declined to discuss the settlement struck by the firm and its former client. But he did say that "at the end of the day, your everyday broker and many investment professionals did not understand the risk associated with these complex derivative mortgage investments."

The independent directors who served on the Regions Morgan Keegan mutual funds' board also may have misjudged the risk.

The board includes Jack R. Blair, nonexecutive chairman of DJO Inc., an orthopedic equipment company; Albert C. Johnson, an independent financial consultant; W. Randall Pittman, chief financial officer of Emageon Inc., a health care information systems company; Mary S. Stone, a certified public accountant and University of Alabama professor; and Archie W. Willis III, a former first vice president at Morgan Keegan who is president of Community Capital, a financial advisory and real estate development company.

Another director, James Stillman R. McFadden, is chief manager of McFadden Communications, a commercial printing concern that does work for Regions Bank, government filings show. Between 2005 and June 30, 2007, Mr. McFadden's firm received $2.46 Million in revenue from the relationship, or 5 percent of his company's sales during the period.

Because most of the directors did not own shares in the devastated bond funds, they have not been hurt by their sharp decline. Among the six independent directors, only two owned shares in the funds as of last September: Mr. McFadden owned between $1 and $10,000 worth, while Mr. Willis owned between $10,001 and $50,000 worth, according to regulatory filings.

The Morgan Keegan spokeswoman said that none of the directors would be available to discuss their oversight or ownership of the funds.

Now that the Wish Fund's complaint has been settled, Ms. Ceaser-Hudson can carry on the organization's work.

Among the wishes that the charity recently granted were a family trip to Yellowstone National Park for an 8-year-old girl, Mary Ann, and her family and a meeting earlier this month between 14-year-old Samantha and Miley Cyrus, the Disney television star who plays Hannah Montana. (The Wish Fund did not release last names of recipients.)

In mid-December, Ms. Ceaser-Hudson set up a shopping spree, complete with limousine transportation, for Sabe, a 3 1/2-year-old handicapped boy with leukemia. Last April, Andrew, 17, got his wish to meet Peyton Manning, the Indianapolis Colts quarterback, and to attend a team practice. The teenager, who had cancer, died a week after his wish was granted.

"What we do try to do is make every single wish a quality wish, no matter what the cost," Ms. Ceaser-Hudson said. "We try to make it something the family and child will always remember."

From The New York Times, December 30, 2007 © 2007 The New York Times. All rights reserved. Used by permission and protected by the Copyright Laws of the United States. The printing, copying, redistribution, or retransmission of this Content without express written permission is prohibited.

***

Chapter 5
Understanding the Sub-Prime Debacle

The first step in understanding the impact of the "sub-prime debacle" is to understand that the problem morphed into far more than a "sub-prime" issue. The crisis began in sub-prime loans. It rather quickly evolved into a broad credit crisis that almost brought the world into another great depression. We are still feeling the impact of what became a world-wide crisis. The very attempt to apply the "sub-prime debacle" label to the problem was a deflection of blame away from Wall Street, the primary villain in the frightening collapse.

When the mortgage market first began to tremble in 2007, the immediate cause was deemed to be the "sub-prime" market. Even as the crisis escalated, Wall Street types, ever in search of scapegoats, continued to blame "sub-prime" products and everyone involved with the origination of the product. Mysteriously, they found no blame in their incessant clamoring for more products, which could be slapped into poorly conceived securitizations supported by suspect ratings which Wall Street controlled, and aggressive sales techniques to force this financial garbage onto unsuspecting investors. The same techniques were used to broaden the market into CDOs (Collateralized Debt Obligations), CLOs (Collateralized Loan Obligations) and other products that were almost never suitable for typical retail investors. For those same investors to be adequately warned and prepared for future assaults on their financial security, it is important to understand the historical background of what occurred.

The financial press produced a barrage of stories about what caused the "collapse" of the sub-prime mortgage market and who should bear the blame. It is usually the case when a financial "correction" occurs, for pundits and self-appointed "experts" to focus everywhere except on Wall Street when trying to identify the real culprits. Blaming Main Street or even back-street mortgage originators for what happened in the sub-prime market is like blaming the neighborhood drug peddler for the drug abuse epidemic in America.

[131]

An examination of the origins and development of the sub-prime mortgage market makes clear the important and dominant role Wall Street underwriters have played in creating, nurturing and growing the sub-prime market, and, ultimately, their role in abusing borrowers and investors. Of course, along the way, "the Street" made a bundle, and has NEVER had to answer for the incompetence, deception and outright fraud which were perpetrated.

A sub-prime loan is just what the name implies: a loan made to a borrower who has poor credit or some other flaw that would disqualify them from getting a conforming loan (i.e., a loan which would be sold by the originator to Fannie Mae [FNMA] or Freddie Mac [FHLMC1]).[5] Historically, FNMA and FHLMC provided liquidity to the conforming mortgage markets. In simple terms, loans were made and securities were issued using the loans as collateral to ensure payments of principal and interest to investors who purchased the securities. Investors would not only rely on the collateral, but also on the guarantee provided by FNMA and FHLMC, both of which functioned as Government Sponsored Enterprises and have since become costly wards of the government. The originating financial institution would then, after selling its product to FNMA or FHLMC, have cash and could make another loan. The creation of massive liquidity was a driving force in the growth of the mortgage market and in the price escalation of real estate. The improvement in technology and the incessant search for sources of profit by Wall Street led to seeking other types of collateral and the growth of the Asset-Backed Securities (ABS) market.

Credit card debt, trailer park loans and jumbo loans (above the dollar amount for the loan to be eligible for delivery to FNMA or FHLMC) were used. Portfolios of recording artists were even used as collateral for the creative originators of ABS products. Mortgages eventually became the primary collateral of choice. Let's look at how the sub-prime market originated and at what happened as the market blossomed and boomed.

---

[5] It is beyond the scope of this book to explore the detailed workings of FNMA, FHLMC or other government housing agencies or programs.

[132]

The first ABS was issued in 1995. This is a relatively new market, and the development of that market parallels and was a huge contributing factor to a boom in real estate prices. From 1995 until 2003, loan issuance went from $1.2 Billion to almost $500 Billion and then, according to Thompson Financial, rose to over $850 Billion in 2004. By 2007, well over $3.5 Trillion in ABS had been issued, including both public and private issues.

The January 2005 SEC definition of ABS stated:

> **The term Asset-Backed Security is currently defined in Form S3 to mean a security that is primarily serviced by the cash flows of a discreet pool of receivables or other financial assets either fixed or revolving, that by their terms convert into cash within a finite time period plus any rights or other assets designed to assure the servicing or timely distribution of proceeds to the security holders.**

The Wikipedia explanation of ABS noted that: "A significant advantage of asset-backed securities is that they bring together a pool of financial assets that otherwise could not easily be traded in their existing form." The Wikipedia statement was true and the liquidity provided by numerous ABS structures was a boon to many market participants and investors. However, as with all too many good concepts and practices, greed on the part of some originators overwhelmed virtue.

One banker who was selling sub-prime loans to a Wall Street underwriter tells an interesting story which illustrates the nature of the fraud and deceit being foisted onto unsuspecting investors. Our banker friend had sold millions of dollars worth of loans, most of which were not originated by his "federally insured institution." Instead, almost all the loans he sold to Wall Street were originated by "wholesale" originators who then sold their product to our banker friend. He, in turn, sold the product to Wall Street. One of his loan officers informed him that a home backed by a mortgage which had been purchased from a "wholesaler" had a "problem." He asked for details and was told that the home "had no roof." Wanting to be fair, the banker picked up the telephone and called his close friend on Wall Street and informed him that the home backing a loan which had been sold to the firm a few days earlier had a "ventilation problem." Instead of being told the loan would be sent back, the Wall Street investment banker replied: "No problem, we're trying to build this deal up as large as we can. We'll just use it as collateral, and the investors will never know the difference."

This story and very similar versions were repeated tens and scores and hundreds of times during the rapid expansion of the ABS market.

As this "we'll take anything" policy on the part of Wall Street underwriters encouraged mortgage brokers at the street level to create loans out of thin air, the fraud process escalated. Wall Street would often use known inferior quality as a justification for paying a lower price but would, generally, still gobble up the production. Lenders were made aware, sometimes indirectly and sometimes bluntly, that Wall Street would take virtually "anything" and those lenders complied. They gave Wall Street anything and everything.

One way Wall Street was able to sell mass quantities of ABS product was by selling credit enhancements, which caused investors to focus less on the underlying collateral and more on the widely trumpeted credit enhancements. The Bond Market Association publication, describing ABS securities, noted that more than 90% of issues were at AAA level and that the credit worthiness was derived from sources other than the ability of the originator to pay, or of the underlying assets.

Let's look at the typical structure of an ABS originator's deal, done using a special purpose vehicle (SPV). The only functional reason for the existence of the SPV is to buy the assets and then securitize them. The SPV is bankrupt proof and cannot be successfully attacked. It normally sells the collateral (loans) to a trust, which then issues the interest bearing securities. Almost all deals involve some form of credit enhancements, which boost

[134]

ratings and give investors a high enough comfort level to buy the securities. This was especially true in the rising real estate market. Wall Street marketers of the product usually made passing reference to the rising value of the underlying collateral, but usually stressed the credit enhancements more than the value of the collateral.

Wall Street created various types of enhancements and consistently emphasized to their pension fund and other institutional, as well as individual, buyers that the quality of the collateral was of less importance than the value of the enhancements. Thus, what really mattered in protecting investors was the quality of the credit enhancements. Let's examine some of the credit enhancements implemented by the fertile minds on Wall Street.

In a typical deal, one type of enhancement would be over-collateralization. This meant that if the deal was to be for $200 Million, it would actually contain $202 Million in loans or collateral, with the "extra" $2 Million segregated or set aside as the over-collateralization or "O/C" account. These loans would be used to absorb losses before any of the other collateral in the account was exposed to risk.

In addition, there would be private mortgage insurance (PMI) which normally was issued on all loans with a loan-to-value ratio greater than 80%. A major form of credit enhancement included in many deals was loan guarantee insurance. Here, the issuer would stress that an insurance policy was set up to cover a certain percentage of loss within the portfolio. This was over and above the PMI coverage issued on individual loans. In a typical policy, coverage applied to between 5% and 10% of the total. In other words, if the coverage was for 5% of a $200 Million deal, then $10 Million of the loans could default and the policy would protect the security holder (investor) from any loss.

However, there were often limitations on the coverage of the loan guarantee insurance. These limitations were buried deep into a long and complicated prospectus and were seldom, if ever, drawn to the attention of buyers. For instance, the coverage would often not apply to "fraudulent" loans. This meant that if the insurer determined that a loan was fraudulent, they would simply refuse to provide coverage for that loan, leaving the investors to bear the loss. The determination of what was fraudulent was often a unilateral decision left to the company issuing the policy. An investor could not even get criteria or any details from the insurance company as to why an individual loan was deemed fraudulent.

In connection with the loan guarantee policies, the following information should have been provided to investors but often was not:

(a) Mortgage loan level information regarding insurance claims and insurance proceeds paid by the insurance companies for defaulted mortgage loans.
(b) Examination of claims which were rejected and reasons for rejection by the insurance company.
(c) A thorough explanation of criteria used by the insurance companies in the determination of fraud and misrepresentation as a reason to reject coverage on a defaulted loan.
(d) Examination of defaulted mortgage loans with regard to their loss and recovery experience by zip code in order to cheek for property appreciation.

There was another selling "feature", while not a direct credit enhancement, that was something Wall Street firms would emphasize. This added feature was having a "name" servicer be responsible for administering the deal (i.e., collecting principal and interest and forwarding payments which would go to investors). The servicer was also responsible for notifying late payers, collecting from stragglers, and instigating and following through on foreclosure and bankruptcy.

Another important feature used to lure investors and to provide a high comfort level in the complex structure was to have a

[136]

big name trustee, usually one of the major New York banks, accept payments from the servicer and forward them to investors. That big name trustee would also be responsible for tabulating data which came from the servicer.

Obligations of the trustee generally included obtaining and reporting the number and amount of claims submitted under the loan guarantee policy. This was often done only partially, if at all. The trustee should always take the appropriate action to obtain the information required to be furnished to investors. Again, this was, all too often, not done.

The trustee was theoretically responsible for looking out for the interest of the investors. In fact, the trustee generated huge income from Wall Street and often put the underwriter's interests above those of the investors.

All of these enhancements and features combined to form an attractive and alluring package for investors. Rating agencies, relying on the combination of collateral credit enhancements and features, placed credit grade ratings on billions of dollars worth of ABS. Real estate prices went up. The defaults were minimal. Initially, all the gears meshed and everyone was happy. Then problems began to develop. Greed overpowered common sense. Wall Street let it be known that it would take virtually any loan. The process and system began to spiral out of control.

One of the complicating factors was that servicers were oftentimes subsidiaries, or captive participants, of the Wall Street issuer/underwriter. The same is often true of the originator sources. The Wall Street firm would use its mortgage company to acquire loans from "federally insured institutions." They stressed in the prospectus given to investors that the originators were "responsible parties" and that the underwriter knew the source of the loans. However, underwriters generally failed to disclose to investors that the vast majority of loans were coming from unregulated wholesalers. They also failed to disclose that little or no due diligence was done to check the quality, or lack thereof, of the loans that went into a particular deal.

The sub-prime market exploded as mortgage originators realized Wall Street would take anything. Delinquencies spiraled upward and foreclosures soon contributed to putting the financial system on the verge of collapse. Sub-prime loans grew by leaps and bounds as all caution in making loans was thrown to the wind. Wall Street drove this explosion. It was Wall Street's voracious appetite, the yawning jaws shouting out "we'll take anything, bring it on, bring it on" that led to the fraud, abuse and the bumbling, stumbling explosion of a market that went way beyond its reasonable bounds.

Another unfortunate factor was the huge number of adjustable rate sub-prime loans that were included in many ABS deals. This fact was also, generally, played down in Wall Street's sales pitches, with the disclosure of the percentages of adjustable rate loans limited to the fine print. As interest rates began to rise, adjustments took place and many borrowers could not meet the higher payments. This led to greater delinquencies and ultimately to far more defaults. As defaults increased, investors were left holding the bag.

The originating Wall Street firms tried to insulate their own position by wholesaling to smaller regional securities dealers many of the highest risk tranches of ABS products. Many of the regional dealers lacked the technical expertise to properly evaluate the securities, or to explain to their buyers the results of limited and inadequate analyses. The regional dealers salivated over the prospect of big spreads, and, relying on prodding from originators, sold the ABS product. They took the big spreads and ended up scrambling to explain, to many of their customers, how they both were hoodwinked by the big boys on Wall Street. Ultimately, Wall Street, like a typical drug dealer, couldn't resist dipping heavily into their own product resulting in the demise of Bear Stearns, Lehman Brothers and others.

The regional dealers often rely on Bloomberg analytics to structure their presentations to individuals and institutional investors. Bloomberg was founded in 1981 by Michael Bloomberg, who went on to become Mayor of New York City. As an information services news media company, Bloomberg provides a wide range of features, including a combination of information, analytical electronic trading and communication tools. Bloomberg is an excellent global news, television, radio, internet, magazine and book publishing operation. However, the analytics Bloomberg offered in the ABS area, during this period, were simply inadequate. Its stature as a publisher did not qualify Bloomberg to be the preeminent analytical source for the kinds of complex and sophisticated analyses required in analyzing ABS products.

This is because the Bloomberg analyses assumed no credit losses would occur to the security being analyzed. Failure to disclose this fact would be a grossly negligent misrepresentation or omission, if not fully revealed and explained to potential buyers. Instead, the state of the art analysis for this type of product was provided by Intex Solutions, Inc. According to the Intex web site, the company noted that it was in the business of providing the most accurate, timely and comprehensive data models and related software for the structured fixed income market. In touting its ABS analytical capabilities, Intex noted that structured transactions were replete with nuances that could, and did, have a great impact on cash flows. Intex made clear that even AAA rated structures with razor thin margins need careful attention and demand accurate analysis. The Intex web site provided clear evidence that, to be accurate and reliable, ABS analytics must go far beyond the minimal calculations provided by Bloomberg. Any securities dealer pushing the sale of ABS products based on Bloomberg analytics was clearly offering incomplete, inaccurate, and what might be highly misleading, information. Yet, literally billions of ABS products were sold by uninformed regional dealers, while Wall Street turned a blind eye to what was happening.

An article in *Fortune Magazine,* written by Bethany McClain, described what fed the ABS problem:

> "These products exploded in popularity in recent years because investors, including pension funds and insurance companies which must mostly buy investment grade rated debt had a voracious appetite for them."

That, in turn, encouraged the historic increase in sub-prime lending.

Here again, the emphasis was misplaced. Very few products are "bought," even in the so-called sophisticated world of institutional investors. The reality is that products are SOLD! This is, almost always, true in the world of retail investors. These products are cleverly packaged and aggressively marketed by Wall Street. Direct contact with buyers is made by articulate sales people. The harder ABS products were sold, and the more profit Wall Street made, the more Wall Street continued to seek out the collateral to feed the machine. The vicious cycle expanded and accelerated.

Another element in the grand scheme of the process was the role of the ratings agencies. Since investors were looking to buy investment grade rated debt, getting an appropriate rating on the product was critical. Moody's net income went from $159 Million in 2000 to over $700 Million in 2006, in large part, from fees generated in ABS deals. The rating agencies were hardly disinterested bystanders. Much like Wall Street analysts during the tech boom, the ratings agencies did not act as impartial analysts. The ratings often relied on illusory credit enhancements and persuaded investors to purchase staggering volumes of ABS product.

The problems with sub-prime loans were not restricted totally to residential loans. On March 6, 2007, Standard & Poor lowered ratings on four classes of commercial mortgage pass-through certificates from Credit Suisse First Boston Mortgage Securities Corp. This proved to be the tip of a large iceberg. Suspect commercial properties, just like suspect residential properties, were hastily thrown in as collateral for securitization, given that Wall

Street securitizers knew they could be sold to anxious investors trained by Wall Street sales people to acquire such product.

Deterioration in the market became rampant. A random sample, conducted by one mortgage company, indicated that 20% of loans that went into early payment default (EPD) were damaged, unoccupied properties (the loans were fraudulent to begin with). Even the slightest due diligence by the Wall Street originator would have uncovered these problems. One Wall Street originator was known to do due diligence on 5% of the loans in a deal. If 20% came back as "bad loans," those 20% would be taken out of the deal. One could, and should, reasonably assume a similar experience with the other 95%. However, the firm would do no more due diligence and would place all the remaining 95% into the collateral pool.

EPD was an area in which servicers participated in a massive fraud. In most early payment default situations, the originator would be required to repurchase loans it had originated and sold to the underwriter as collateral. However, there usually was a 90 day to one year limitation on the EPDs. This meant that if a loan defaulted within the first 90 days (or whatever period was selected) the originator was required to take back the loan. Since often times the originating mortgage company was a subsidiary of the underwriter, this would have created a problem for the corporate hierarchy of the Wall Street underwriter. By having the servicer advance principal and interest beyond the cutoff period for early payment default, it would avoid this consequence.

When the servicer advanced the money for the 90 day cutoff period, the fictional appearance was maintained that the loan was good. When the cutoff period passed, the loan would go in default and the loss would be taken by the investor rather than having the bad loan put back to the originating mortgage company. This type of fraud on investors amounted to billions of dollars. The entire problem was greatly exacerbated by the fall in real estate prices. This drop also served to emphasize the link between real estate price escalation and the ABS market. Neither, regulators or legislators, took any meaningful action. The sub-prime mess broadened. Additional ABS products were used to carve up the financial futures of retail investors and the campaign of greed and avarice marched onward.

Key Points:
➢ Wall Street actions were the primary source of the mortgage market collapse beginning in 2007.
➢ Some Wall Street "credit enhancements" were primarily designed to sell products, not to protect investors.
➢ Major Wall Street firms took advantage of smaller regional dealers as well as end purchasers.

***

HORROR STORY

Sidney currently resides in a Florida convalescent home, suffering from the early stages of dementia.

As he was descending into a darkening fog of dementia, his broker, affiliated with a major Wall Street brokerage firm, began to make all decisions in Sidney's account.

The broker's firm was well aware of Sidney's deteriorating conditions but exercised no supervisory oversight of the broker and the activities within the account. The broker was allowed to roam free in his dealings with Sidney. The broker knew that Sidney's mental health was in decline yet never made appropriate changes in Sidney's account.

The broker had a history of six prior customer complaints and, based on that record, should have been subject to heightened supervision. No such supervision was ever imposed.

When Sidney's account was first opened, in 2006, the investment objective was "long-term growth." Sidney was 71 at the time, retired and expected to live on his retirement funds.

In 2008, as Sidney's condition worsened, the broker had Sidney agree to change his objective to "speculation." He then began a pattern of aggressive trading using margin.

[142]

Sidney was not an experienced trader and had never owned or traded any stocks using margin. He totally lacked any understanding of the risk ramifications of using margin. The funds being used were irreplaceable retirement monies.

As a result of being sold highly speculative stocks, on margin, and due to a complete lack of any meaningful supervision, Sidney lost over 90% of his retirement funds. The considerable expense of his care is now a financial burden being covered by his family. He lost over $1 Million dollars while the brokerage firm pocketed over $450,000 in commission income.

★★★

Chapter 6
The Great CMO Heist

It is helpful to understand Wall Street's endless desire to sell those products that pay the highest spreads or commissions. The structured finance products that led to much of the market chaos, and ultimate collapse, in 2008 offered huge enticements to sellers of the products. The highly profitable (for sellers) and highly risky (for buyers) structured finance products did not rise up out of nowhere. They evolved and were nurtured by the most creative minds on Wall Street.

The first mortgage-backed security (MBS)[6] was brought to the market under the banner of the Government National Mortgage Association (GNMA) in 1970. The so-called Government Sponsored Enterprises (GSE) soon followed with the Federal Home Loan Mortgage Corporation (FHLMC), bringing its MBS product out in 1971. The Federal National Mortgage Association (FNMA) joining the party in 1981.

Initially, the creation of these pass-through products benefited virtually everyone. The mortgage markets became more liquid. Areas of low housing demand and with excess cash deposits provided housing support for areas with greater demand and less cash availability. The products were fairly simple. If you owned 1% of a pool of loans, you got 1% of the principal and interest payments which were "passed-through" from the underlying mortgages. Even some of the initial innovations were positive, designed to meet the desires of insurance companies to own products with long-term maturities and the needs of financial institutions to meet short and intermediate-term investment needs.

However, Wall Street's fixed-income specialists soon saw an opportunity to make more money than could ever have been imagined in the relatively sterile days of treasuries, corporate bonds and municipal bonds.

---

[6] Refers to securities backed by mortgages which include pass-through securities, mortgage-backed bonds, mortgage pay through securities and collateralized mortgage obligations (CMOs).

Under the guise of "serving the needs of diverse investors" the Collateralized Mortgage Obligation (CMO) was born. The first CMO was created in 1983. The structural architects were hailed, much the same in the fixed-income world, as the God-like "tech" analysts were in the world of equities and IPOs.

The same underlying mortgages would be diced, sliced, and carved up, down, and sideways with the underwriters taking their piece at every turn. These were no longer simply "pass-through" securities but each deal was divided into multiple classes (or tranches), which is the French word for slices. The initial deals would have 3 to 5 classes but by the early 1990s there would be 30 or more classes in each deal. The Wall Street creativity machine was in high gear and the big profits were just beginning. The evolution was rapid and, in hindsight, stupefying. The early three-class deals were based on sequential payments. The first class would have a lower coupon and an earlier maturity. Interest and <u>all</u> principal payments would go to the first class until it was paid off. The subsequent classes would get interest only — no principal — until the first class was fully paid off. Thus, the first class would have a short life span, with the second, third and subsequent classes having intermediate to long term lives. The initial structures were fairly tame and, as the Bloomberg[7] print out shows below **(Illustration 1)**, offered a steady cash flow —clean and predictable.

---

[7] All illustrations are from Bloomberg's website and are reprinted with the permission of Bloomberg, L.P. Bloomberg, L.P., founded in 1981, is an information services, news and media company, servicing customers in 126 countries around the world. Bloomberg, L.P. provides a combination of information, analytic, electronic trading and communication tools. In addition to providing the BLOOMBERG TERMINAL, Bloomberg L.P., has global news, television, radio, internet and magazine and book publishing operations.

Illustration 1

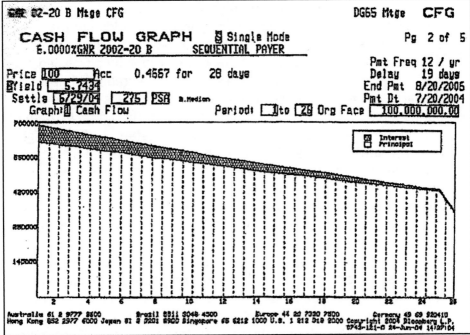

Consider a few of the early, and still <u>relatively</u> benign, innovations. The goal was to enhance predictability in the costs and the returns of these investments. This led to the creation of Planned Amortization Classes (PACs). These PACs would have a band of prepayment speeds. Prepayment assumptions were, and are, based on the Public Securities Association (PSA) and Constant Prepayment Rate (CPR) prepayment models. CPR was the initial measurement and PSA was created to account for slower prepayments in the early life of most mortgages. PSA assumes 0.2% of the pool prepays in the first month and increases by 0.2% in each month until the 30th month when the prepayment rate levels out at 6% CPR. The CPR is a percentage prepayment rate which relates the percentage of the outstanding balance prepaid on an annual basis. For comparative purposes, 0.2% CPR in the first month would be equal to 100% PSA. After month 30, 6% CPR is assumed to equal 100% PSA. A 12% CPR would equal 200% PSA.

Early marketers knew little about the real risks of the products they were selling. Those secrets were closely guarded by the upper management and trading gurus who doled out the assumptions they wanted salespeople to use. Amid great fanfare, the creation and distribution of this product took on a frenzied pace. Many early investors, mostly banks, thrifts and credit unions learned the hard way about the perils of extension risk. This led a few bankers to refer to "CMO" as meaning "Count Me Out." The damage heaped on many smaller institutions was substantial. Few sought help or redress, not wanting to be embarrassed in their local community. This passive reaction encouraged the best and brightest on Wall Street to intensify the charge to capture this available money by hook or by crook. The race for more complex and more profitable products for Wall Street was in high gear.

The damage touched individuals as well as institutional investors. Small financial institutions and unsuspecting individuals would be told a product had a 4 year "maturity." A change in market conditions would bring prepayments to a screeching halt and, virtually overnight, change the product into one with a 15 year life. The investor would then be holding a substantial loss and many small institutional investors were required to "mark-to-market," even if they did not sell the instrument. As you can imagine, the impact on individuals was, and is, oftentimes even more devastating. An individual would be sold a "tricky" class as if it were an alternative to CDs or near cash instruments. Later, when they wanted to liquidate, they would find that the CMO they had been sold was worth far less than what they had paid for it. **Illustrations 2** and **3** are examples of the consequences of "extension risk" gone awry. Extension risk occurs when the average life of the security becomes longer. When interest rates rise, fewer mortgage holders prepay their mortgage, which increases the life of the security.

Illustration 2

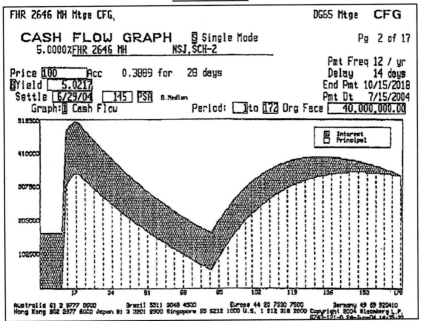

Illustration 3

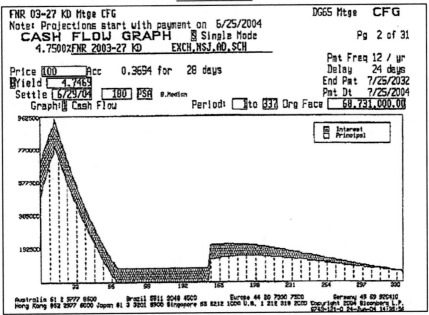

These graphs can, of course, be confusing to the untrained eye. The important fact to gather from them is that substantial early payments came to a screeching halt. Had they been maintained, they would have resulted in a short maturity. This slowdown, or "extension," converted these products from short term to long term holdings.

Compared to the steady predictability of the instrument in **Illustration 1**, other CMO classes often came to represent roller coaster rides that were seldom appropriate for any investor, especially the uninformed investor. The term "uninformed" includes virtually all but the most sophisticated institutional investors. The products proved to be far beyond the ability of small banks, credit unions, pension funds and other "institutional investors" captured by the charming tales of Wall Street spin masters. Many paid with their jobs.

Illustration 4

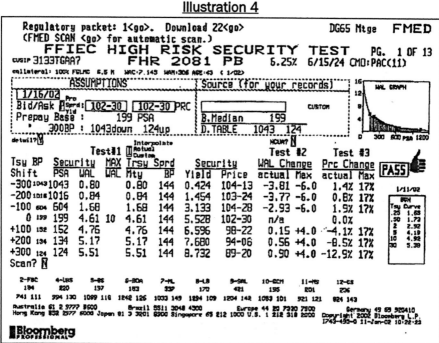

As shown in **Illustration 4,** there were three Federal Financial Institutions Examination Council (FFIEC) tests which had to be passed for a security to be purchased by a financial institution. The first test required that a specific security could not, at purchase, have a weighted average life[8] of more than 10 years.

Secondly, the weighted average life could not shorten more than 6 years or lengthen more than 4 years given a 100/200/300 basis point shift in interest rates.

The third test involved price volatility stating that the price could not change more than 17%. These FFIEC tests became the gospel for regulated, institutional investors. It was obvious that most buyers did not know what they were doing in this area and the horror stories became commonplace. To protect these "sophisticated" investors, which Wall Street picked on like fish in a barrel, regulators took action and made FFIEC test compliance a regular part of every financial institution's examination. If an examiner found a security had been purchased which flunked the test, the bank could be forced to sell the security.

There is no longer an automatic liquidation requirement, but the purchasing institution has the burden of describing what they bought and why they bought it. If they can't meet that requirement to the satisfaction of the examination team, the institution will still, at the least, face a regulatory "write-up." Banking regulators acted to protect the banks. No one, as usual, took any meaningful steps to protect individual investors. Even on the institutional side, if a broker dealer sold securities to a bank which violated the FFIEC

---

[8] This is the standard measure of risk in mortgage backed securities products, as opposed to most other types of securities, which use maturity. Generally, securities with a longer maturity, or "average life," will be more volatile and have greater price variance than those with shorter maturities. Most mortgage-backed securities have 30 year stated maturities (there are also 15 year and a few other final maturity products in the marketplace but they represent a distinct minority), but given the monthly principal payments, defaults and refinancing, most of the cash flow will be received much earlier. The final, stated maturity date will not change, but the prepayment rates do change leading to a variance of the weighted average life.

test, the regulatory consequences fell on the buyer. As usual, the lax regulators of the sellers took no action over the industry they were "regulating."

This chart can appear to be a complex of meaningless statistics. However, cutting to the core requirements of the three tests provides revealing background about the complexity of Wall Street's handiwork.

Wall Street did not view the FFIEC test as a deterrent, but instead, took it as a challenge. Major firms began to structure product to be "on the edge." Given the base test, the security would, at the time of purchase, pass the test. Within a few short months, the same security would fall off the edge, leaving the frustrated banker as yet another victim of extension risk. It was clear, in hindsight that investors needed to run prepayment scenarios at slower or faster speeds than those required to meet or pass the base test at the time of purchase. Because the major firms were able to circumvent this standard test with "on the edge" structures, bank regulators dropped those hard-line tests and told banks to establish their own limits for the three FFIEC tests and justify their limits in their own investment policies. Again, the seller could say, "It was OK when I sold it," and leave the buyer to deal with the negative fallout.

Let's trace a specific example from beginning to tragic end. A small financial institution purchased a Federal Home Loan Mortgage Corporation (Freddie Mac or FHLMC) CMO. The instrument had a 5% coupon with a Weighted Average Coupon (WAC) of 5.43% and a Weighted Average Maturity (WAM) on the underlying collateral of 350 months. The original projections on the security showed a Planned Amortization Class (PAC) Bond of 147 to 202 PSA. The zero (0) base used for this security which is based on the consensus of primary dealers was 186 PSA. This indicated a bond equivalent yield of 6.013%, a dollar price of 98 3/32 and an average life of two years. On those PSA assumptions, this would produce a principal window of 5/04 - 11/09 on 30 year collateral.

A regional dealer wanting to be conservative, rather than accept the Wall Street rhetoric without question, ran the security at 125 PSA, which was 61 PSA below the consensus median. This produced a principal window of 5/04 - 2/13 which produced an average life of 2.9 years. The rate shock analysis run using the FFIEC test showed that a 300 basis point rate increase would produce a bond equivalent yield of 5.475% with a 5.18 year average life. Rates down 300 basis points would produce an 8.23% bond equivalent yield and an average life of 0.57 years.

The banker purchased this security based on all the projections created by the originating primary dealer and passed on in good faith by the broker with the small, regional dealer. Two weeks after agreeing to the purchase, the banker got a shock when he checked on his purchase and found it listed, not as a PAC bond but, as a "non-sticky jump" (NSJ). The original average life purchase went from 2 years on the purchase date to 16.5 years on settlement date! The buyer was informed that he had a loss in the security of approximately 18 points, or almost $180,000 on an initial purchase of $1 Million.

The number and types of classes would be comical if they did not represent such a costly smokescreen for investors. **Illustration 5** is a Bloomberg listing of CMO class types. The point is investors never receive the information necessary to evaluate risk. It was impossible, and still is, for the average and even a very "sophisticated investor" to know the meaning of these terms, much less, the wordings of the products they were used to describe. The complex information for CMOs became a forerunner for the far more complex, and potentially catastrophic, structured finance time bombs that followed.

If you are totally confused and frightened by this chapter just remember one lesson - <u>DON'T EVER BUY THIS KIND OF PRODUCT</u>! The products are complex but the lesson is simple. Do not let yourself be <u>sold</u> the Wall Street stories. Some products are made for selling; some are made for buying. CMO's and their offspring have no place in the portfolio of an individual investor.

Illustration 5

```
CLASS CMO                                              PO60 Mtge   MTG

Bloomberg           CMO  CLASS  TYPES        (YELLOW = BLOOMBERG TYPE)
CMO

 1) AD     Accretion Dir.    21) INV  Inverse Floater   41) SC   Structured Coll
 2) AFC    Available Funds   22) IO   Interest Only     42) SCH  Scheduled Pay
 3) ARB    Ascending Rate    23) LIQ  Liquidity         43) SEG  Segment
 4) AS     Accel Security    24) MEZ  Mezzanine         44) SEMI Semiannual Pay
 5) CALL   Call Option       25) MR   Mandatory Redemp. 45) SEQ  Sequential Pay
 6) CAM    Controlled Am.    26) NAS  Nonaccel Security 46) SJ   Sticky Jump
 7) CMPLX  Complex           27) NPR  Non-paying Resid. 47) SM   Scheduled Mty
 8) CPT    Component         28) NSJ  Non-sticky Jump   48) SNSTP Senior Strip
 9) CSTR   Coll. Strip Rate  29) NTL  Notional Prin.    49) STEP Step Rate Bond
10) DCALL  Date Callable     30) PAC  Planned Amort.    50) STP  Prorata Prin Str
11) DLY    Non-Zero Delay    31) PEC  Payment Exchange  51) SUB  Subordinated
12) DRB    Descending Rate   32) PO   Principal Only    52) SUP  Support
13) EDC    Extended Delay    33) PT   Pass Through      53) SWAP Swap
14) EXCH   Exchangeable      34) PUT  Put               54) TAC  Targeted Amort.
15) EXE    Excess P&I        35) PZ   Partial Accrual   55) TBD  To Be Determined
16) FLT    Floater           36) R    Residual          56) W    Wtd Avg Coupon
17) FTV    Fix to Variable   37) RSTP Ratio Strip       57) XAC  Index Alloc.
18) HAZ    Hazard Bond       38) RTL  Retail            58) XRESET Extended Reset
19) HB     Hard Bullet       39) SB   Soft Bullet       59) Z    Accrual
20) IAN    Index Amort       40) ..   ....
Enter:     (number) <Go>   or  MTG (descriptor) <Go>   Ex:  MTG AD <Go>
Australia 61 2 9777 8600    Brazil 5511 3048 4500    Europe 44 20 7330 7500  Germany 49 69 920410
Hong Kong 852 2977 6000 Japan 81 3 3201 8900 Singapore 63 6212 1000 U.S. 1 212 318 2000 Copyright 2005 Bloomberg L.P.
                                                                  H146-173-0 06-Apr-09 10:02:59
```

Used with permission of Bloomberg L.P. Copyright © 2012. All rights reserved.

Few brokers can adequately explain to investors the subtleties and nuances of these numerous classes. Most don't even try. They rely on the assumptions provided to them by traders and managers and set sail to convince investors to "trust" their assumptions and conclusions.

Freddie Mac (FHLMC) FHR 2594 lists 228 classes in a single deal, with all 228 classes, taking their cash flow off the same instruments. Who, among investors, could hope to accurately analyze such a structure? Investors, institutional and individuals alike need to be protected from the Great CMO heist. Literally, millions of dollars have been lifted from investors and transferred to the overstuffed pockets of Wall Street.

As a result of the financial meltdown, we have been in an era of low interest rates. No one can accurately predict when interest rates will rise again, but they will. Below is an example of a more recently issued CMO which is exposed to the same extension risks as the older CMOs, described above.

[154]

Illustration 6

```
                     66      FHR  3990  GN              3.5%  1/15/42  ADV:<PAGE>
                    <GO> 3137AL3U1  CMO:PAC-2(22)        [ 174  252  5/12] NO Notes
  65 FGLMC 4.5 M       4.912(313)35 WAC(WAM)AGE MAY12                    88 <Go>
 <GO>
MAY  1mo  195P 11.7  1/30/12:   5,490,000 │ next pay  6/15/12 (monthly )  30/360  Cashflows
'12  3mo  213  12.8                        │                               created  5/12/12
     6mo  182  10.9  5/15/12:   4,884,935 │ rcd date  5/31/12 (14 Delay) 1stProj  6/15/12
     12mo 167   9.4                        │                               Collat:  18 Pools
     Life 197  11.8  factor 0.889787820000 │ accrual  5/ 1/12- 5/31/12
 5/22/12              30/360 DSCNTNG        YIELD   TABLE
 B.Median          +300bp107  +200bp134 +100bp209   0bp376  -100bp673  -200bp798  -300bp827
 Vary        L1
 PRICE      .52    107 PSA   134 PSA   209 PSA   376 PSA   673 PSA   798 PSA   827 PSA

                 DEAL: CALL FEATURE: 1% Deal cleanup is not considered in analytics for this bond.

 100-16 │   3.473      3.462      3.197  │  2.874  │  1.926      1.403      1.373


 AvgLife   (15.88)   (12.45)    2.06       1.01      0.40       0.30       0.30
 Mod  Dur   12.00     9.94      1.93       0.97      0.40       0.30       0.30
 DateWindow 6/27-    9/23-     6/12-      6/12-     6/12-      6/12-      6/12-
            2/15/29  12/15/25  7/15/18    9/15/13   11/15/12   10/15/12   9/15/12
 Spread II +140/AL  +158/AL   +290/AL   +269/AL   +180/AL    +130/AL    +127/AL
           MAY12 APR MAR FEB JAN12                      Treasury Curve = BGN   9:33
 CALL Provision 195 267 177 145 151p      6mo  -1-  -2-  -3-  -5-  -7-  -10-  -30-
 NOT Modelled  11.7 16.0 10.6 8.7  9.1c    0.14 0.18 0.29 0.39 0.74 1.17 1.74 2.86
 Parity Px 99.854                    Format# 1-YT          B
 Australia 61 2 9777 8600 Brazil 5511 3048 4500 Europe 44 20 7330 7500 Germany 49 69 9204 1210 Hong Kong 852 2977 6000
 Japan 81 3 3201 8900    Singapore 65 6212 1000    U.S. 1 212 318 2000    Copyright 2012 Bloomberg Finance L.P.
                                            SN 204962 CDT  GMT-5:00 H21S-118-1 17-May-2012 09:33:41
```

The weighted average interest rate of the mortgage pool for this security is 4.912%. The average life of the security in the base case is 1.01 years. If interest rates rise 2%, the average life extends to 12.45 years and to 15.88 years if interest rates rise 3%.

Times have changed. Market conditions have changed. However, the ever aggressive presence of Wall Street's marketing powers is the overriding constant. Individuals and smaller institutional buyers continue to be sold CMOs and other complex structured products. The embedded risks and massive exposure to even small market changes are seldom fully revealed and almost never adequately explained.

A letter I received a few years ago from a frustrated broker summed up the problem:

> I have been in the institutional fixed income
> business for years but have become so frustrated
> with the shenanigans of Wall Street in the
> structuring of CMOs, and other structured finance

products, that I have decided to hang up my license. These products have become a vehicle for primary dealers to reward their best accounts and to foist the trash off on small dealers, financial institutions and individuals.

This letter proved to be a harbinger of far worse things to come!

An individual investor needs to remember only three words when it comes to CMOs and their many complex offspring – COUNT ME OUT!

Key Points:
➤ Complex CMOs are rarely suitable for individual investors.
➤ Don't trust Wall Street's analysis and predictions about future performance of these products.

Chapter 7
Structured Finance Securities

Leave it up to Wall Street to devise the mother lode of complex, fee generating products: structured finance securities. One Wall Street observer referred to these structures as the "Pac-Man of investor portfolios." CMOs were the starting point. In hindsight, CMOs are tame and innocent forerunners of what became the Frankensteins of Wall Street. These descendants of CMOs were numerous and diverse but they all shared one common characteristic, extremely high risk. The full scope of that risk was hardly ever revealed to investors. Investing is dangerous enough for the individual investor when investments are made in stocks, bonds and plain vanilla mutual funds. Investors should grasp the important fact that these products are constructed for the profiteering benefit of Wall Street architects and not for the benefit of investors.

The more complicated the product, the less transparent the risks (and the fees) are to the investor. These extremely complex securities are so opaque that they are understood by very few of the people on Wall Street involved in creating them and even fewer who are involved in aggressively selling them. Obviously, many on Wall Street had little understanding of the embedded risks in these securities since structured finance products were a major contributor to the 2007-2008 debacle. Even institutional investors could not figure out many of the subtle risks of these securities and relied, to their detriment, on their trusted Wall Street advisors.

The Wall Street surprises continue. In June 2012, J.P. Morgan Chase announced a $2 Billion Dollar loss in structured product. Estimates of the total losses have already been raised to over $6 Billion and the investigation is ongoing. Jamie Dimon, the highly acclaimed CEO of J.P. Morgan Chase, testified before Congress, in June of 2012, that the trading strategy was "not carefully analyzed." Dimon, casting blame on JP Morgan traders, declared that the traders "did not have the requisite understanding of the risk they took." In March and April of 2012, Dimon offered a different excuse, claiming the losses were due to temporary market movements. The "let's blame the market" refrain is heard often from Wall Street dice rollers when abstract concepts go away.

According to public perception, J.P. Morgan Chase houses some of Wall Street's most brilliant minds. If they can't get it right, why should the average investor ever fall prey to a Wall Street sales pitch to become an owner of complex, structured products?

Securitization is the method utilized by Wall Street to create the pools of assets that are used in the creation of structured finance securities. The process of issuing securities backed by pools of assets is referred to as securitization and the underlying assets are said to be securitized. To create structured finance securities, Wall Street created pools of risky assets which included mortgage loans, subprime loans, collateralized debt obligations, aircraft leases, credit cards, trust preferred securities, REITs and synthetic securities of credit default swaps to name a few. The risk and the performance of structured securities are determined by the pools of assets upon which these complex securities are based. Structured securities have a high degree of illiquidity due to the customized nature of the investments.

In the world of structured finance, the different investment classes of securities are created by tranching. A tranche is one of the classes of securities contained in a particular structured transaction. As previously stated, the word <u>tranche</u> is French for slice. All of the tranches, taken together, make up the capital structure of the particular issue. The tranches are identified in the structure by letter (Class A, Class B, Class C, Class D, etc., depending on the number of tranches). Cash flow is generally paid to the tranches sequentially, from the most senior tranche to the most subordinate. The tranches suffer losses in the reverse order, sequentially, with the most subordinate tranches taking on losses first and serving as a line of protection for the more senior tranches. Each tranche has a bond credit rating which can range from AAA, for the most senior tranches, to B or unrated for the most junior tranches.

[158]

The following chart, from the Commercial Mortgage Securities Association (CMSA), is illustrative of the risks and returns of the various tranches in a transaction.

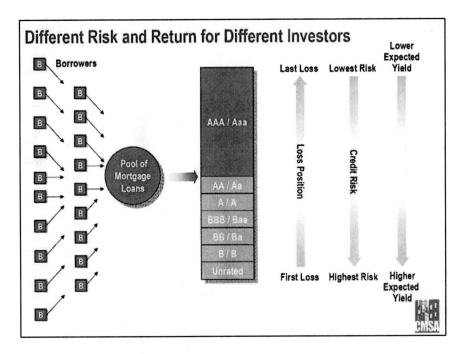

These complex structured finance securities were rarely suitable for the average investor when sold as individual holdings. In an effort to maximize profits and avoid suitability issues, some Wall Street underwriters placed these toxic securities in bond mutual funds sold to unsuspecting investors. Full disclosures of the magnitude of risks embedded in these securities were almost never made, and the investor had no way of monitoring the deterioration of the assets underlying these securities. Wall Street pushed the "diversification" of mutual funds containing these products. They failed to disclose that the funds were highly leveraged and a small drop in value of underlying collateral could wipe out the lower tranches.

The Bloomberg security description page for the Kleros subordinated tranche provides a look into the complex nature of these products. A cursory glance should be enough to convince the "average" investor to steer clear of these types of highly risky structures.

KLROS 2006-5A E Tranche

Underlying collateral – collateralized loan obligations (CLO), asset-backed securities (ABS), residential mortgage-backed securities (MBS) and related synthetic securities.

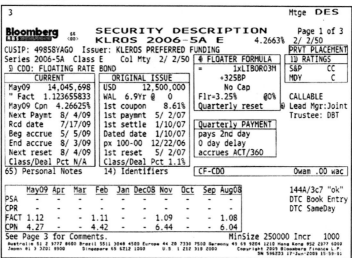

LISTING OF TRANCHES IN THE KLEROS STRUCTURE

	CF Class	Orig(000)	Cpn	OWAL	Factor	Cusip	Description	Group Description
1)	A1	1,020,000	0.541	6.87	0.9822	49858YAA3	FLT	ALL collateral
2) •	A2	80,000	1.366	6.95	1.0000	49858YAB1	FLT	ALL collateral
3) •	A3	40,000	1.466	6.95	1.0000	49858YAC9	FLT	ALL collateral
4)	B	28,500	1.536	6.95	1.0000	49858YAD7	MEZ, FLT	ALL collateral
5) •	C	8,000	2.416	6.95	1.0877	49858YAE5	MEZ, FLT	ALL collateral
6)	D	2,500	2.566	6.95	1.0906	49858YAF2	MEZ, FLT	ALL collateral
7)	E	12,500	4.266	6.95	1.1237	49858YAG0	FLT	ALL collateral
8)	SUB	8,500	1.690	0.00	1.0000	49858YAH8	SUB, EXE	ALL collateral

According to the listing of tranches above, when the SUB tranche sustained losses and was wiped out, the E tranche was next in line to suffer a complete loss and be wiped out. The SUB tranche only provided 0.007% of loss coverage to the E tranche, which made owning the E tranche precarious at best.

Wall Street thrives on selling complicated products to unsophisticated and unsuspecting investors who cannot adequately evaluate them. ANYONE, including institutional investors, investing in structured securities must be very careful, but the non-sophisticated investor should <u>never</u> invest in a structured finance security.

<u>Key Points:</u>
➢ Structured finance products are far too complex for individual investors.
➢ Don't trust Wall Street "expertise" to protect your interests in these products.
➢ Don't be tricked into buying funds which own these complex products.

Section 3

Pension Funds

Chapter 8
Victimizing Pension Funds

Individuals are not Wall Street's only victims. Pension funds, corporate treasurers, school districts, charitable foundations and many others have felt the sting of abuse.

Many Americans are counting on pension funds to contribute to, or make up all of their retirement funding. Their confidence may well be misplaced in many instances.

Most public funds are defined benefit plans. This means that the city, county or other public body is obligated to pay the beneficiaries, whether or not the earnings are there to justify the payments. Shortfalls must be made up by raising taxes, increasing fees and other sources of revenues or by reducing costs and services. Taxpayers are on the hook, usually without having any clue as to the potential liabilities they face. Reducing benefits is not an option.

Most corporate plans are defined contribution plans. In these situations, the risk falls to the beneficiaries who, like taxpayers, generally have no idea that the future payment stream may well cease to exist.

Let's focus on just the pension funds. Many are being ripped off by Wall Street and most of them don't even know it. The beneficiaries have even less knowledge about what is being done to them.

The stories are frightening and the potential losses and government liability could well rival the savings and loan debacle and/or the mortgage crisis. We have already seen smatterings of the potential problem. The tip of the financial iceberg is but a fraction of what lies below the surface.

Every dollar is important to pension funds and to the beneficiaries of those plans. A recent study by the Pew Research Center shows a 2010 gap, just for the 50 states, of $1.38 Trillion between what they owe and what has been set aside. While the greatest shortfall has been the result of unfunded liabilities, poor recommendations by pension consultants and shoddy investment planning and abuse have also been major contributors to the problem. Cities, counties and other public entities are, in many instances, in even worse shape. Three California cities, Stockton, San Bernardino, and Mammoth Lakes, recently sought bankruptcy protection.

The City of San Diego's problems from several years ago were widely publicized. Diann Shipione, one of the fund directors for the City, started asking questions about the fund's relationship with its investment consultant, Callan Associates. Frustrated, she concluded, "I was trying to do my fiduciary duty by throwing out a few questions, but there's no way to know what's really going on." This problem goes back to the early 2000s. It is typical of the kinds of problems still taking place in the pension fund world.

In San Diego, Callan, in its role as "consultant," for which it was being paid $200,000 per year, recommended six large cap growth managers to the city. Interestingly, all six were purchasing consulting services from Callan and were members of the Callan "Institute." Big money was flowing from the managers to Callan. Not only was Callan siphoning off huge fees, but their recommendations raised questions. One of the selected managers ranked in the bottom 8% of its peer group category for the previous three years.

Pension fund problems are not new, but they are ongoing. In 2002, UBS Paine Webber, Inc. paid over $10 Million to settle a case with the Nashville & Davidson Metropolitan Benefit Board. The firm was accused of charging excessive fees, understating the risks in the portfolio and failing to provide full and adequate information about investment strategy recommendations. This dispute also centered on the firm's performance as **consultant** to the city's pension fund. The consultant acts as a "gatekeeper," selecting the managers who will be awarded lucrative contracts to manage a funds' investment. Paine Webber had received soft dollar, or directed brokerage fees for over 10 years.

According to an August 2002 article in Fortune magazine, Paine Webber was taking in over $1 Million a year in trading commissions from the Nashville account. A proposed new plan aroused suspicions of Nashville decision makers who initiated an investigation. The inquiry led to the filing of the claim that was later settled.

The Nashville case highlighted problems which continue to plague pension funds. The same Fortune article noted that, "By some estimates as much as $1 Billion a year is being siphoned from the plans in inappropriate dealings."

The City of Chattanooga also reached a settlement with its pension consultants. Former Mayor, and now U.S. Senator, Bob Corker was quoted in the Chattanooga Free Press following the settlement:

> **We felt like the city had been wronged. This is certainly going to be a huge benefit for taxpayers.**

Ted Siedle, president of Benchmark Financial Services and a former SEC lawyer, advises pension funds on a variety of money management issues. He has long questioned the role of "consultants" to pension funds, raising serious conflict of interest issues. Siedle, who has been widely quoted in articles in Forbes, the New York Times and elsewhere on consulting firm conflicts and abuses, identified seven ways consultants financially benefit from the pension funds they advise:

1. **Annual contractual fee or retainer.**

2. **An agreed upon fee (in addition to an annual retainer) for special projects such as manager searches or brokerage studies.**

3. Brokerage fees from the fund's money managers related to the accounts they manage for the fund.

4. Additional brokerage fees from other accounts of the fund's managers.

5. Additional "search fees" for terminating managers and finding new managers.

6. Cash payments from the fund's managers, including venture capital and real estate managers or the custodian.

7. Marketing consulting fees from managers (including how managers should market themselves to consultants) and conference attendance fees where managers can meet pension clients of the consultant.

As is obvious, the pension consulting business is highly lucrative!

Siedle concluded:

> "As a result of all the above devices, the fees pensions actually pay, directly and indirectly, to consultants are ten or more times greater than the amount they think they are paying. It is an elaborate ruse and pension officials almost universally have refused to look behind the facade to examine what is really going on...pension consulting fees today are dramatically understated."

The performance results - impacted by excessive fees, gross mismanagement and blatant conflicts of interest - are abysmal. The tax payers don't get off unscathed. The Miami Herald reported that:

> "The $55 Million Hallandale Beach Police and Fire Pension Fund's returns are so rotten,....that the city and state together this year are having to kick

> in almost $3 Million to shore up the fund. That
> works out to $244 per taxpayer."

Several Wall Street firms, attracted by the opportunities for
large fees, jumped into the "consulting" game. The roles of several
of the firms have been questioned and led to major disputes. In
Florida alone, a large number of pension funds entered into
settlements over consultant related issues. The SEC summarized
its findings in a 2009 Order:

> From at least 2002 through 2005, Merrill Lynch,
> through its pension consulting services advisory
> program, breached its fiduciary duty to certain of
> the firm's pension fund clients and prospective
> clients by misrepresenting and omitting to
> disclose material information. Merrill Lynch's
> pension fund clients came to it seeking advice in
> developing appropriate investment strategies and
> in selecting money managers to manage the
> assets entrusted to their care. In providing such
> advice, Merrill Lynch failed to disclose the facts
> creating the material conflict of interest in
> recommending clients use directed brokerage to
> pay hard dollar fees, and in recommending the
> use of Merrill Lynch's transition management
> desk. In addition, Merrill Lynch made misleading
> statements to the clients served by its Ponte
> Vedra South, Florida office ("Ponte Vedra South
> office") regarding its manager identification
> process. As a result of the above conduct, Merrill
> Lynch violated Section 206(2) of the Investment
> Advisers Act of 1940 (the "Advisers Act"). In
> addition, Merrill Lynch failed reasonably to
> supervise its investment adviser representatives
> in the Ponte Vedra South office with respect to the
> provision of advisory services to its Consulting
> Services clients. Finally, Merrill Lynch violated
> Section 204 of the Advisers Act and Rule 204-
> 2(a)(14) thereunder by failing to maintain records
> of the offer or delivery of disclosure statements.

A Forbes article published back in 2004, entitled "A Bribe By Any Other Name," questioned the activities of consultants who collected fees from funds for rendering advice while also collecting from the money managers they referred into the funds:

> "Anybody who remembers how analysts insisted they weren't influenced by their firm's underwriting assignments or how auditors insisted that tax consulting assignments never clouded their judgments, maybe a bit skeptical of such claims."

Omission is a recurring theme in pension fund dealings. A recent filing set out typical claims:

> As a result of the omission of these material facts, the Plan was deprived of the ability to accurately understand the relationship between it and the Consultants, and as a result the Plan was unable to make educated and fully informed decisions,...More importantly,...was able to take advantage of its relationship with the Plan by creating undisclosed fee arrangements that enabled them to reap significant commissions, fees and other benefits, and gain control over all of the transactions concerning the management of the Plan. The foregoing arrangements created by Respondents created material conflicts of interest between the best interest of the Plan and those of Respondents because...and Consultants were thus not independent consultants, which the Plan believed they were. Based upon the "soft dollar" arrangements recommended and implemented by..., Consultants were able to select "aggressive" or "active" managers for the Plan who would be faithful to a trading strategy consistent with...demands and Consultants' interests, rather than consistent with the Plan's objectives and needs. This "aggressive" or "active" strategy was only beneficial to...and Consultants because by reason of the "soft dollar" arrangement, they

[170]

> received substantial and excessive commission income.[9]

Soft dollar arrangements are a favorite device of consultants to gain entry into a fund. "We'll do it for free," is the opening line. These firms know that soft dollar arrangements almost always result in excessive payments, not cost savings. The SEC defines soft dollar practices as arrangements under which products or services, other than execution of securities transactions, are obtained by an advisor from or through a broker dealer in exchange for the direction by the advisor of client brokerage transactions to the broker dealer. In simple terms, soft dollars are just commissions generated by securities transactions. Obviously, this provides an incentive for the consultant to select broker dealers who will pursue an investment strategy which generates more, rather than less, active trading within the account.

Pension fund problems know no geographical boundaries. A Dutch pension fund filed claims asking for damages in excess of $300 Million against a Goldman Sachs affiliate. The claim, vigorously denied by Goldman Sachs, alleged improper investments in sub-prime related products in 2007.

Analyzing a pension fund case is different and more complex than analyzing a typical situation involving an abused investor. Most funds made, and are still making, money. They generally are not producing negative returns. In the Nashville case discussed earlier, the city made money but showed that the excessive fees it was paying belonged to the city workers not to the "trusted advisor." The action was brought, not because the overall account suffered losses but, because the funds were being charged excessive fees and received advice which lowered returns. Proper analysis requires, not just looking at portfolio performance but, every detail of the consulting contract and the arrangements with individual

---

[9] ...a more "passive" or indexed investment strategy would have reduced the commissions earned by...reduced investment advisory fees and it would have increased the Plan's returns. This should have been the true goal of an "independent" or "objective" consultant.

[171]

managers, the selection process, disclosures (or the lack thereof) and compliance with written investment policies.

Identifying and tracing the money flow is a daunting, but revealing, challenge. Following the money trail down a labyrinth of twists and turns is comparable to chasing skillful money launderers!

The individuals who deal with pension funds are generally among the highest compensated marketeers at every major Wall Street firm. Transparency? There is almost none. The key to successfully pursuing the funds that belong to firemen, policemen and garbage workers whether retired or looking forward to retirement, is "old-fashioned hard work."

If you are a pensioner, or are expecting to receive a future pension, demand that "hard work" from those responsible for protecting the plan's best interests.

<u>Key Points:</u>
➢ Don't assume that all is well with your pension fund.
➢ Get involved. Ask questions. Follow fund performance. Question those in charge.

Section 4

FINRA

Financial Industry Regulatory Authority

* * *

HORROR STORY

A divorcee in her 70s who lost $1 Million filed a FINRA arbitration claim as called for by the account opening document the broker dealer required her to sign. After all of the usual discovery and other procedural happenings, and after settlement discussions were broken down, the matter proceeded to a hearing.

The night before the hearing, the Chairperson of the arbitration panel approached the victim's counsel in the lobby of the hotel. The strong odor of alcohol coming off the Chairperson's breath could be smelled from 10 feet away. After a few introductory comments, the Chairperson asked, in a loud and threatening tone, why the Claimant would sue "such a fine firm?"

The victim's lawyer informed the Chairperson that, given the improper approach and the inappropriate comment, a request that the panel could rule impartially would be entered when the arbitration began. This was done and the panel members all stated, on the record, that they could and would rule impartially. The hearing moved forward.

The Chairperson consistently ruled against the investor's interests as the hearing proceeded. It was so obvious that the victim asked counsel why even bother to continuing with this "kangaroo court?"

On the second day of the hearing, the Chairperson approached both attorneys representing the victim. The Chairperson asked how many cases they had filed against this company and how much money they expected to make.

The Respondent filed a Motion to Dismiss the case prior to the conclusion of the hearing, arguing that the applicable state statute of limitation barred the claim. FINRA claims are not governed by state statutes of limitations but by a six-year eligibility limitation which is part of the FINRA rules.

The Chairperson, the only lawyer on the panel, persuaded the other panelists to join him in granting the Motion to Dismiss on the morning of the fourth day of the hearing.

The ruling was clearly contrary to the applicable FINRA rules regarding Motions to Dismiss.

The panel added insult to injury by indicating that, contrary to the requirement of the rule, no written explanation would be provided. The Claimant expressed frustration, but no surprise, given what had occurred over the course of the previous three days.

Shockingly, the Chairperson stated for the record that the applicable statute of limitations began to run from the date of her first purchase and NOT from the date of her last purchase, which occurred less than a year from the time her case was filed. This meant that the claim would have been barred well before the investor was even aware that a claim existed. There were numerous purchases made between the date of the first and last purchase. It is preposterous to assume that multiple purchases totaling hundreds of thousands of dollars would have been made AFTER the victim knew there was a potential cause of action. No other court or arbitration panel could have come to the same conclusion as this panel did. Such a finding does not comport with how statutes of limitations are applied in matters involving ongoing fraud and concealment of the fraud.

FINRA, in its training materials (NASD Panel Member Training Guide. 2002 Version 1.2 at page 58), agreed with positions taken previously by the Director of Arbitration:

> **For example, although a customer purchased stock 10 years ago, you might find there are allegations of ongoing fraud starting with the purchase, but continuing to date within six years of the date the claim was filed.**

The panel in this case clearly ignored this guide. Yet, the victim was left with no options.

There is no provision under the FINRA rules which allowed for a reversal of the clearly erroneous ruling. The investor's only recourse was to file a judicial appeal, which given an overall feeling of frustration and disgust, she chose not to do.

[175]

Claimant's counsel did make FINRA aware of the Chairperson's outrageous conduct and improper rulings and asked that the Chairperson be removed from the FINRA pool of arbitrators. FINRA informed counsel that a "secret" investigation would be conducted which would not include speaking to Claimant or to Claimant's counsel. FINRA stated further that all findings would be confidential. Neither the investor, nor her counsel, has ever heard another word from FINRA on the matter.

✶✶✶

Chapter 9
What is FINRA?

"FINRA maintained, as its top priority, to protect investors..." This quote from FINRA accompanied its 2010 Annual Report. A number of facts belie this statement and should alert investors to the cruel fact that FINRA is far more dedicated to protecting the interests of its members than the interests of public investors.

A large book could be devoted to exploring the sloppiness, ineffectiveness and ethical shortcomings of FINRA. Exploring these topics to their full extent would go beyond the scope of this book. The message of this book as it relates to FINRA is simple. Do not take seriously FINRA's claim to "protect investors." FINRA is a trade association fueled, primarily, by the contributions of its members. FINRA never forgets its real mission, first and foremost, is to protect the interests of that membership.

Most people are unaware that FINRA was previously known as the National Association of Securities Dealers (NASD), which told the world that the organization was a trade association. Financial Industry Regulatory Authority sounds like a government regulatory body. However, it is, in fact, the same trade association operating under a high sounding protective moniker.

In excerpts from the 2010 FINRA Year in Review and Annual Financial Report, the high level employees of FINRA are hardly paid like regulators.

These high payments have not always been well received, even by some of the member firms whose fees represent the primary source of reliable income for FINRA. Objections usually come from smaller FINRA firms who often feel that FINRA actions are driven by the interests of the larger member firms. An excellent summary of this situation was posted by Alden Burcher on August 5th, 2011 in RegBlog[10]:

> How much is too much to pay a financial regulator? A number of critics have posed this question to the Financial Industry Regulatory Authority (FINRA), the country's largest independent securities regulator which oversees over 4,500 financial brokerage and securities firms.
>
> According to its most recent financial report, FINRA paid eight members of its ten-person board of directors more than a million dollars each in 2010. Cumulatively, the FINRA board members earned more than $12.7 Million, up from the $10.6 Million that the board received in 2009.
>
> FINRA executives earn significantly more than the chairs of comparable government agencies, whose compensation is set by the Executive Schedule. FINRA Chairman and Chief Executive Richard Ketchum earned more than $2.6 Million in 2010. By contrast, Securities and Exchange Commission (SEC) Chair Mary Schapiro earned only $165,300 last year, while Federal Reserve Chair Ben Bernanke earned $199,700.
>
> However, Schapiro, herself a former FINRA chief executive, received approximately $3.2 Million in her final year at that agency before being nominated to her current position with

---

[10] *FINRA Executive Compensation Challenged by Member Firms* *http://www.law.upenn.edu/blogs/regblog/2011/08/finra-executive-compensation-challenged-by-member-firms.html*
[178]

the SEC by President Obama in January, 2009.

One FINRA-regulated brokerage firm, Amerivet Securities, filed an action against the organization in August, 2009, alleging excessive executive compensation, among other claims. A District of Columbia Superior Court denied FINRA's motion to dismiss in March, 2011. Because Amerivet seeks only further inspection of FINRA's corporate books, and not damages, the court ruled that FINRA cannot claim immunity as a self-regulatory organization.

Amerivet's legal action is still pending, with no trial date yet set.

Interestingly, a large portion of FINRA's income comes from its own proprietary trading, which has not always gone well, and is hardly an expected priority of a regulator.

FINRA's net income for 2010 was $54.6 Million and $48.6 Million for 2009. These relatively modest earnings followed the $696.3 Million in losses suffered by FINRA in 2008. As a result of the losses, FINRA's Board of Governors decided to shift FINRA's strategy to one that was less volatile.

Ironically, very few FINRA panels have found many of the types of investments which cost FINRA millions in its proprietary trading activities in 2008 to be unsuitable for the average retail investor.

FINRA touts its Board of Governors as having more public members than securities industry members (11 out of 21). Looking at the background of many of the "public" members is revealing. For example, James E. Burton is part of California Strategies LLP, which is said "to provide an expert perspective on complex financial and business activities..." Earlier in his career, he served as Chief Executive of the World Gold Council and led the development of the first gold-backed Exchange Traded Fund (ETF).

Richard S. Pechter retired as the Chairman of the financial services group at Donaldson, Lufkin & Jenrette (DLJ) where he oversaw $2 Billion in annual revenue. He commented in a New York Times article that:

> "I was at the very top of Wall Street, the very top firm, the very top guy."

John W. Schmidlin is the former Chairman of the Technology Council at J.P. Morgan Chase & Company.

William H. Heyman is Vice-Chairman of the St. Paul Travelers Group. Prior to that, he was Chairman of Citigroup Investments and earlier served as a managing director of Salomon Brothers.

It strains one's credibility to believe that these highly compensated "public" members bring the perspective of retail investors to their positions.

***

HORROR STORY

Bloomberg

Wall Street's Captive Arbitrators Strike Again
By William D. Cohan - July 8, 2012

A set piece of Voltaire's 18th century masterpiece, "Candide," is a scene in which the British, after losing a battle, execute one of their own admirals "pour encourager les autres."

The analogy may be a bit heavy-handed, yet in many ways it fits what Finra -- the Financial Industry Regulatory Authority, Wall Street's self-regulatory organization -- did to three arbitrators who, in May 2011, had the temerity to find in favor of a customer in a securities arbitration against Merrill Lynch, the nation's largest brokerage and a unit of Bank of America

[180]

Corp. After awarding the estate of the customer more than $520,000 -- a large amount by arbitration standards --Finra heard from unhappy Merrill executives and fired the arbitrators, two of whom had many years of experience.

"You mete out justice, and then you get slapped in the face," one of the fired arbitrators, Fred Pinckney, told me in an interview.

The matter began in December 2009, after Robert C. Postell, of Alpharetta, Georgia, and his wife, Joan, filed an arbitration claim against Merrill Lynch for more than $640,000 plus attorney's fees. Postell, who had a successful automotive-safety-equipment business, claimed that his Merrill broker failed "to adequately monitor" his accounts, according to a publicly available copy of the Finra arbitration summary. The Postells also asserted claims of "breach of contract" and "breach of fiduciary duty" against Merrill. Not surprisingly, the brokerage, through its attorney, Terry Weiss, of Greenberg Traurig LLP, in Atlanta, denied the Postells' claims.

Finra Waiver
Anyone who works on Wall Street or has a brokerage account must agree, from the outset, that any financial claims made against their employer or broker will be adjudicated not in the courts but in an arbitration process overseen by Finra, a private organization that derives the bulk of its $1 billion in revenue from the Wall Street companies that are its members. This upfront agreement by millions of Americans to submit to a Finra arbitration process -- which I experienced firsthand in the 2003-2004 -- constitutes one of the largest ongoing abdications of legal rights in the U.S., and nobody seems to be bothered enough to rectify it.

(To make matters worse, Mary Schapiro, the chairman of the Securities and Exchange Commission, was previously head of Finra, whose board awarded her a $9 Million bonus when she left that post in January 2009.)

In May 2011, the Postells' arbitration claim was heard in seven sessions over four days by the three Finra-appointed arbitrators: Ilene Gormly, the chairperson and a former compliance executive at a commercial bank; Daniel Kolber, a securities-law attorney and the founder of Intellivest Securities Inc., a small Georgia investment bank; and Pinckney, an Atlanta attorney. The arbitrators are paid about $200 a day.

According to Pinckney, at the final hearing, on May 6, the arbitrators were informed that Postell had committed suicide in February. His estate, along with Joan, would be the claimants in the arbitration and the beneficiaries of any award. Also during the final hearing, according to Pinckney, Weiss, Merrill's attorney, sensed that he was losing the case and repeatedly "exploded at the panel," accusing the arbitrators of being biased in their views and rulings against Merrill. The panel took a break, called Finra executives and explained Weiss's accusations. With <u>Finra</u>'s blessing, the arbitrators decided to proceed to final arguments and conclude the matter. Soon thereafter, the arbitrators found in favor of the Postells and awarded Joan and her husband's estate $520,000 in damages.

Culled Roster
According to Pinckney, about two months later, Kolber got what Pinckney called a "black spot letter" from Finra explaining that the private regulator periodically examined its "roster" and culled people from it. "As a result," Kolber's letter read, "please be advised that you are no longer being listed as an active member of Finra's dispute resolution roster of arbitrators."

Then, in January 2012, Gormly, who has about 20 years experience as an arbitrator, got her "black spot letter." In June, Pinckney was notified that he was relieved of his duties. According to Pinckney, Finra executives denied a request from Kolber for a meeting. Then, Gormly sent a "whistle-blower" letter to the SEC, describing the situation. She hasn't heard back.

"I told her that she will probably be waiting until hell freezes over," Pinckney said.

Pinckney is pretty disgusted by this turn of events, especially since there were no grounds to appeal the arbitrators' decision in the Postell case and no appeal was filed. Nothing about what the three arbitrators did was ever questioned, except by Weiss, the Merrill lawyer who saw his case being lost. Pinckney said his fellow arbitrators weren't looking for reinstatement or compensation. He contacted me to share his story because he was so outraged that Wall Street has the ability to exact revenge on arbitrators in a quasi-judicial system where it already holds most of the cards anyway.

"It's unbelievable that they would take such an experienced panel and get rid of it," Pinckney said. "To me, this undermines the credibility of the entire Finra process – I didn't say kangaroo court – but when you have three well-credentialed people, doing their job, and there were no meritorious grounds for an appeal, and we get handed the 'black spot' – and not all at once – it makes for a pretty cheap novel."

Where does it all end? Will there really be zero accountability for bankers, traders and executives who caused a calamitous financial crisis, or the collapse of MF Global Holdings Ltd., or who were gambling with $350 billion of depositors' money, or who were manipulating Libor, or for those who are further cheapening a Wall Street-administered arbitration system that already reeks of injustice?

(William D. Cohan, a former investment banker and the author of "Money and Power: How Goldman Sachs Came to Rule the World," is a Bloomberg View columnist. The opinions expressed are his own.)

Reprinted with permission granted by the author of this article, William D. Cohan.

***

While the above information is important for investors to know about FINRA and that FINRA's priority is loyalty to its broker dealer members, it is more relevant for investors to know how investors have fared in disputes with FINRA members. As described, investors' only option to formally pursue claims against broker dealers, in most situations, is FINRA's Dispute Resolution forum.

William Francis Galvin, Secretary of the Commonwealth of Massachusetts, in testimony before the U.S. House Subcommittee on Capital Markets, Insurance, and Government Sponsored Enterprises, stated on March 17, 2005:

> **"The term 'arbitration' as it is used in these proceedings is a misnomer. Most often, this process is not about two evenly matched parties to a dispute seeking the middle ground."**

FINRA Dispute Resolution arbitration results demonstrate surprisingly low win rates for investor claimants. The FINRA website shows that in 2011, only 44% of claims brought by investors resulted in any recovery for the investor. Keep in mind that, in some of those "winning" claims, the final recovery amounted to a minuscule percentage of the damages sought. However, the award still ended up in the "win" column for investors.

In a 2007 study entitled, <u>Mandatory Arbitration of Securities Disputes Statistical Analysis of How Claimants Fare</u>, Edward S. O'Neal, Ph.D. and Daniel R. Solin demonstrated that if an investor finds himself in an arbitration proceeding, the percentage of claim he can expect in a win is a declining function of the amount requested in the case. For example, their data concluded that Claimants in a case requesting over $250,000 can expect to recover approximately 12% of their losses against a large broker dealer. This is compared to claimants in arbitration against top 20 brokers, who face an expected recovery of approximately 28% in claims under $10,000. The study also revealed that the size of the brokerage firm in arbitration has an impact on investor recovery. Below is a chart from the study showing statistics of claimant recovery:

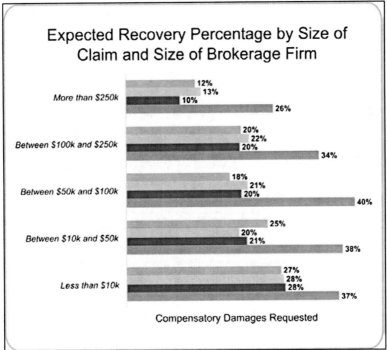

It is shocking to see that investors win less than half of the cases taken to a hearing. Of those that win, the percentage of loss recovery is small. It would suggest that investors and their legal representatives are bringing many claims that lack merit. Given the pressure placed on claimants, and that their attorneys almost always work on a contingency basis, it defies common sense to suggest that false claims would be regularly brought before FINRA panels.

Part of the reason for these paltry results stems from the makeup of the arbitration panels. FINRA claims that the arbitration selection process is entirely neutral and random. However, FINRA has long fought attempts to force disclosure of the selection source code process.

There are many brazen problems with FINRA being the sole organization in charge of arbitrating investor disputes with FINRA members. Eliot Goldstein, a Maryland attorney who represents abused investors, recently shared the following story with the authors:

> I have asked a number of FINRA arbitrators I have met over the years (not ones presiding over my cases) if they feel at all chilled at the prospect of issuing a large award in favor of Claimant, or issuing sanctions or attorneys fees against Respondents. Every one of them admitted to me "off the record" that they were indeed always apprehensive about doing so for fear of not getting selected again or being removed as arbitrators from the FINRA rolls. As they see it, FINRA (the national association of broker dealers) is their employer and that is always in the back of their mind throughout the case.

In a 2007 study, Scot D. Bernstein, a California securities attorney, performed a detailed mathematical analysis of a portion of FINRA's arbitrator selection process titled: <u>Stacking the Deck in Arbitrator List Selection: A study in Regulatory Failure and a Practical Look at the Consequences</u>. The study's conclusion was that the arbitrator selection process is quantifiably skewed, providing reason for investors to doubt the fairness of the entire FINRA arbitration process. The details of this study are beyond the scope of this book, but anyone interested in the study can find it on the website for the Law Offices of Scot D. Bernstein - <u>http://www.sbernsteinlaw.com/</u>

If the portion of FINRA's selection process that Bernstein analyzed is as flawed as his analysis demonstrates, can we not assume that the entire process is equally as flawed? If you are ever a disgruntled investor and are considering pursuing a FINRA arbitration claim, you should contact FINRA and ask for an explanation of their arbitrator selection process.

Section 5

How To Defend Yourself

Chapter 10
Demand Your "Investor Bill of Rights"

Generally, state securities regulators have been more aggressive in protecting investors than have FINRA or the SEC. Aggressive enforcement tactics by some state agencies benefiting investors have caused broker friendly legislators at the <u>federal level</u> to call for the elimination of all state securities regulations. Interestingly, it is the same legislators who usually clamor for states' rights that are now pushing for federal consolidation in this area. They are not stupid. They know that they can, with the power of the purse, control the generally malleable federal regulators and industry controlled SROs. Trying to control the often times more idealistic state regulators is a far more difficult task.

State regulators formed a "trade association," the North American Securities Administrators Association (NASAA). The NASAA in 1997 adopted an <u>"Investor Bill of Rights"</u> reminding investors of their rights. The Investor Bill of Rights offers advice and describes ten specific areas in which investors are entitled to protection. The ten rights are set out below, followed by the authors' comments on how they can be most effectively applied to maximize protection to investors:

1. **Ask for, and receive, information from a firm about the work history and background of the person handling your account, as well as information about the firm itself.**
   Some securities firms and many individual brokers are reluctant to provide this information. Investors should demand it. An investor can also seek information from FINRA and from state regulatory bodies. Mysteriously, FINRA records are often not current and are notoriously incomplete. For the latest and most thorough information, always contact state regulators. If there is resistance by the broker dealer to providing any information you want then you are best advised to move on.

2.   Receive complete information about the risks, obligations and costs of any investment before investing.

The key word here is "<u>complete</u>." It is not enough for a broker to say (usually after the fact), that everyone knows there is a "risk." The broker dealer claims to offer, and within realistic expectations should offer, the securities expertise. Complete information should include standard deviation and/or beta of a recommended stock or mutual fund. For bonds, minimal disclosure would include the rating of the specific bond. <u>For complex structured finance products, the ratings alone are wholly insufficient to fully capture the risks embedded in those products.</u> The problem is exacerbated by the fact that the public customer was allowed to even invest in this volatile product market.

3.   Receive recommendations consistent with your financial needs and investment objectives.

This used to be covered by NASD Rule 2310 which covered the "suitability" of a specific security for a particular investor. The security itself had to first be suitable for some investors (reasonable basis suitability) and only then should be tied to a customer's individual financial situation (customer specific suitability). The new FINRA Rule 2111 has been adopted and affords protection for investors regarding recommended strategies including recommendations to "hold." While this may lead to increased enforcement actions by FINRA, it remains to be seen how arbitration panels will deal with the new language.

4.   Receive a copy of all completed account forms and agreements.

An investor is entitled to <u>all</u> documents relating to their account. Keep the documents in a safe place. They should regularly be updated by the broker dealer and be certain that you always have the latest updates. We see a lot of horror stories where the firms mysteriously have documents that the customer does not recall seeing. The firms often send letters stating that the customer should call if they disagree with anything shown on the attached form. Many, if not most, customers pay little attention to such correspondence, giving the broker dealer <u>*carte blanche*</u> to make changes as they see fit to protect themselves at the expense of the customer. If you choose to have an account with a broker dealer, then you owe it to yourself to carefully read and react to any and all correspondence received from the firm.

5. **Receive account statements that are accurate and understandable.**

Check account statements the same way you do your bank statements. Errors are made. Ask for complete explanations about anything you do not <u>fully</u> understand. This is often even more important than the account forms and correspondence a customer receives from the firm.

This involves much more than just checking the balance to see if the account value is up or down. There may be trades reflected in the account that you did not approve. Failure to raise a question may allow the broker dealer to defend itself in a later claim by saying you ratified the unauthorized trade. The broker will also say, in many cases, that you were aware from the statement that you had losses but chose to continue holding the securities. We see case after case where a broker denies, contrary to the customer's position, recommending that the customer "hold." The broker then points to the statement and says the customer clearly knew about the declining value and had an obligation to sell the security.

Broker dealers claim to offer cradle to grave advice in their slick and clever advertising. However, at the first sign of a dispute, they revert to just being an order taker and try to shift all responsibility back to the customer.

Obviously, if that were the case there would be no need for a full-service broker. A discount broker can fill the role of an order taker at far lower costs and without the risk that you will be sold the product paying the highest commission rather than the product that is best for your financial future.

6. **Understand the terms and conditions of transactions you undertake.**

Read all documents, including confirmations, a prospectus, monthly statements and any other item sent by the brokerage firms. Investors have a right to know what is sent to them <u>and</u> to understand the meaning of every obligation they have to the brokerage firm and every obligation which is owed to the investor. Don't be victimized because you trusted the broker to act in your best interest.

7. **Access your funds in a timely manner and receive information about any restrictions or limitations on access.**

If you ever have a problem accessing your funds, ask to speak to a supervisor immediately. If you speak to a supervisor, be sure you take notes of the conversation. Then date, sign and keep your notes. Few, if any, investors ever do this, but this step could someday save your retirement or your financial viability.

8. **Discuss account problems with the branch manager or compliance department of the firm and receive prompt attention to, and fair consideration, of your concerns.**

Develop a relationship with the individual who supervises the broker(s) assigned to your account. Feel free to contact this person directly. If your broker objects to your request to meet and know these people, consider that to be a warning signal and move your account immediately.

9. **Receive complete information about commissions, sales charges, maintenance or service charges, transaction or redemption fees and penalties.**

This information should never be kept from an investor. Without full details, it is impossible to provide a fully "informed consent" to the purchase, sale or retention of a particular security. There are hidden costs, fees and charges in virtually every type of investment you are <u>sold</u> by brokerage firms. That is, in large part, how the industry leaders afford their lavish lifestyles. The best book capturing that concept is the classic <u>Where Are the Customer's Yachts</u>?

10. Contact your state or provincial securities agency in order to verify the employment and disciplinary history of a salesperson and the salesperson's firm; find out if the investment is permitted to be sold; or file a complaint.

If you have been wronged, take action to protect yourself. Know, and use, your rights as an investor. After all, it is your money! Most people, when they feel they have been taken advantage of, reach out to their individual broker. This is <u>NOT</u> always the best and most dependable source. Talk to your CPA, your personal attorney, an independent financial advisor and, depending on the nature of the problem, seek the advice of a securities law specialist.

> **A.E. Dunning wrote:**
> Aaron Burr was a more brilliant man than George Washington. If he had been loyal to truth he would have been an abler man; but that which made George Washington the chief hero in our great republic was the sagacity, not of intellectual genius, but of the moral element in him.

Seek an advisor who, first and foremost, exhibits and practices integrity. That is not always an easy search. The best way to find such an advisor is to seek a fee only professional who is <u>NOT</u> affiliated with a registered broker dealer.

Chapter 11
Forty-One Steps to Financial Self Discipline

The purpose of this chapter is to give our readers suggestions and guidelines for defending themselves from becoming a victim. Though they are listed in the form of "steps," it is important to know that these suggestions need not be executed in any particular order.

1. A dollar saved is truly a dollar earned.

Benjamin Franklin was a great financial advisor. Don't spend foolishly, and that includes avoiding non-productive costs, fees and hidden charges imposed on you by your "trusted financial advisors." Most actively managed funds will under-perform passive funds by at least the total amount of costs. Remember that costs create a negative compounding effect.

Markets give and markets take away. You can't control world events or predict the pattern of gyrating markets. You can control, or at least reduce, many costs. You must insist on transparency. Evaluate. Manage. Control.

2. Be extremely cautious about signing any document declaring you to be a "sophisticated investor."

Beware the words, "it's just a formality and signing this form doesn't really mean anything." The broker will conveniently forget or deny what you were told. The paperwork documentation lives on and will seldom, if ever, be used to help the investor.

3. Passively managed index funds are almost always, over time, better than actively managed funds.

This is now so well established that there can be no reasonable debate to the contrary. There have been endless studies which confirm the futility of active managers' efforts to beat the markets on a consistent basis. These comparisons have been made for years with little change in the consistent pattern. A Vanguard study found that, over a 10 year period, 84% of actively managed U.S. large blended funds and 68% of actively managed small value funds underperformed their index. Bond funds posed an even more stark contrast over the same time frame, with 95% underperforming their indexes. Historically, the funds that outperformed in a given year failed to maintain that performance level. A Barclay's Global Investors study showed that, over a 5 year period, only 41.6% of large cap funds that beat the S & P the previous year repeated that performance in the next year. After 3 years, only 9.7% were still beating the index.

We tout the preference of passive funds over actively managed funds. However, be advised and forewarned that some passive funds, especially those offered by Wall Street firms, are also guilty of hiding fees and various types of costs. In selecting passive funds, investors almost always get a better bottom line return. However, shop alternatives to be sure that you are not giving a portion of that increased performance back in the form of excessive, unnecessary and, usually, hidden costs.

4. **Have an independent, fee based (as opposed to commission) advisor.**

Be certain that your advisor is not receiving a finder's fee or any form of compensation for "finding" investments for your portfolio. You need to know that the evaluations and advice you are getting are impartial and are driven only by what is in your best interest. Sadly, accountants often fall prey to the siren sound of easy income and become willing "endorsers" of products recommended to their clients. In several states, friendly legislators have passed legislation permitting brokers to split commissions with accountants or attorneys for helping investors "understand and elaborate" investment products. The fact that the "professionals" are splitting fees often taints their advice and, certainly, makes them a questionable source of an "unbiased" evaluation. Avoid even the possibility or appearance of a conflict. Make sure your advisors are in your corner and have only your best interest in mind.

5. **Avoid variable rate annuities.**

Some products are meant for buying. Some products are meant for selling. Variable rate annuities are costly to the buyers but allow the sellers to live high. Avoid them.

6. Limit "play money" to 10-15% of your portfolio.

Most people have, despite their denials, a touch of a gambling streak. They like to "take an occasional flyer." If you recognize the itch; go ahead and scratch it, it but with a pre-determined percentage of your holdings that should never exceed 10-15%. Segregate those funds and monitor the results carefully. If you are like many investors, you will soon see the folly of the approach and fold what is left of the "play" allocation back into the more disciplined part of your investments. It is shocking to see how many individuals are persuaded by an aggressive broker to put a substantial portion of their entire holdings into a single investment or sector. When the "gamble" fails, as it usually does, the brokers usually shout out that they were "just doing what the client wanted."

7. Accept the cruel and harsh reality that Wall Street is not your friend.

As one successful broker shared with the authors, "We are trained to have customers believe we are their friends but taught to remember that our objective is to make as much money off of them as possible."

8. Be a Whistleblower

The Dodd-Frank Wall Street Reform and Consumer Protection Act (Dodd-Frank) amended the Securities Exchange Act of 1934 by, among other things, adding "Securities Whistleblower Incentives and Protections." If any citizen has knowledge of fraud, or other wrongdoing, within the financial industry, the SEC is now providing not only protection to whistleblowers, but incentives as well.

The Dodd-Frank Act whistleblower program will pay awards, subject to certain limitations and conditions, to whistleblowers that voluntarily provide the SEC with high quality original information about a violation of securities laws. The award is paid if the information leads to a successful enforcement of an action brought by the SEC resulting in monetary penalties exceeding $1,000,000. The amount of the award is required to equal 10-30% of the monetary sanction or any related action, such as in a criminal case.

The Dodd Frank Act also provides tough anti-retaliation protections, which permit federal lawsuits for wrongful termination, suspension, harassment, or other discrimination resulting from the whistleblower's reporting to the SEC.

Information and other help from someone who has knowledge of possible securities law violations can be among the most potent weapons in the law enforcement cache of the SEC. Whistleblowers can help the SEC identify fraud and other violations much earlier than might otherwise have been possible through their first hand experience of the circumstances and individuals involved. This can allow the SEC to lessen the harm to other investors and, more efficiently, hold those responsible for unlawful conduct.

The Office of the Whistleblower was established to administer the SEC's whistleblower program. You can reach the Office of the Whistleblower at (202) 551-4790. The following is key information from the Whistleblower question and answer section (FAQ) on the SEC website:

> **1. Who is an eligible whistleblower?**
> An "eligible whistleblower" is a person who voluntarily provides us with original information about a possible violation of the federal securities laws that has occurred, is ongoing, or is about to occur. The information provided must lead to a successful SEC action resulting in an order of monetary sanctions exceeding $1 Million. One or more people are allowed to act as a whistleblower, but companies or organizations cannot qualify as whistleblowers. You are not required to be an employee of the company to submit information about that company.
>
> **2. What does it mean to "voluntarily" provide information?**
> Your information is provided "voluntarily" if you provide it to us or another regulatory or law enforcement authority before (i) we request it from you or your lawyer or (ii) Congress, another

regulatory or enforcement agency or self-regulatory organization (such as FINRA) asks you to provide the information in connection with an investigation or certain examinations or inspections. *See* Rule 21F-4(a).

3. What is "original information?"
"Original information" is information derived from your independent knowledge (facts known to you that are not derived from publicly available sources) or independent analysis (evaluation of information that may be publicly available but which reveals information that is not generally known) that is not already known by us. So if we received your information previously from another person, that information will not be original information unless you were the original source of the information that the other person submitted. *See* Rule 21F-4(b)(1).

4. Can I submit my information anonymously?
Yes, you may submit anonymously. To do so, you must have an attorney represent you in connection with your submission. You must also provide the attorney with a completed Form TCR signed under penalty of perjury at the time you make your anonymous submission. *See* Rule 21F-7.

As an investor, take advantage of the government program to help fight Wall Street. Reporting abuse to the Whistleblower office can make a difference and can be not only personally rewarding, but an important method for protecting other investors.

9. Understand that there is no free lunch.
If it is too good to be true, you can assume, in almost every instance, it is <u>NOT</u> what it is claimed to be. Think Madoff.

10. Don't buy into the nonsense peddled on financial television programs.

The ceaseless stream of "hot tips" and Wall Street jargon is designed to produce profits for brokerage firms and not a source of sound advice for investors. View those shows as entertainment, not as a source of financial direction. In our practice, we see a steady stream of investors who say that CNBC supported what their broker was saying so they "thought it was a good idea."

11. The most important investment decision you can make is how to allocate among asset classes.

Asset allocation is the process of determining the desired mix of asset classes for your financial holdings. Prestigious studies have established that 92% of a portfolio's return is determined by the asset allocation. By comparison, security selection has been shown to be only a 5% determinant. It is critical to find impartial, competent advice to help make the allocation decisions.

You can make these allocations on your own or, have a fee based advisor to help or do the analysis for you. The third option would be to contract with a firm like Index Fund Advisors, Inc. (IFA). The company charges a fee, based on the size of an investor's portfolio, to determine proper asset allocations. The firm then identifies the appropriate PASSIVE INDEX FUNDS which will best achieve the investor's goals. These are low cost funds which reflect market performance. Mark Hebner, founder and CEO of IFA, along with John Bogle, founder of Vanguard, is one of the heroes of providing low cost funds to investors.

In the preface of Index Funds, Hebner's classic contribution to financial enlightenment, he makes his philosophy clear:

> **"I am passionate about my mission to clear the smoke and mirrors designed to conceal the failure of active management. Ultimately, my goal is to lead investors to a highly efficient, tax managed, low cost and risk appropriate index portfolio."**

If more investors became followers of Hebner's simple philosophy, there would be far less financial pain and misery. There would also be far fewer yachts owned by Wall Street practitioners.

[202]

12. Determine appropriate diversification of holdings within each asset class.

Let's assume you allocate 50% of your assets to passively managed stock funds and another 40% to passively managed bond funds. You then allocate 5% to cash, or cash equivalents, and the other 5% to whatever types of "flyers" you select, including individual stocks, metals, or other objects of your interest or curiosity.

The next step is to select the specific investments to hold within each asset allocation. This process is called diversification.

In the example, you would then divide the stock investments into U.S. stock funds or foreign stock funds. Further diversification would be into value versus growth stocks and into a variety of industries. The goal would be to own different types of funds that are not closely correlated.

The same type of low correlation funds should be selected in the fixed-income segment of your holdings. The term correlation simply means the extent to which investments will perform alike, or differently, under similar market conditions.

The old cliché, don't put all your eggs in one basket, is still solid financial advice. Here again, you should seek out competent and impartial advice to help provide a clear, diversification analysis.

13. Reject exaggerated claims of market "seers."

If someone really had the key to the market vault, would they share that secret with you for a commission? Be skeptical. Remember a story as basic as the tortoise and the hare.

Many of these claims are comical entertainment, while some border on blatant fraud. It is often very hard to tell the difference. Seek your entertainment in other areas and remain highly skeptical of these egotistical charlatans.

14. Never invest without a comparative analysis.

Benchmarks are helpful but can be misleading. Make sure you are comparing apples to apples. Brokerage firms often compare performance figures without adequate consideration of relative risks. They also often use benchmarks which are not an accurate reflection of similar risks. Trust, but verify.

15. Understand that costs compound negatively.

Einstein said, "The most powerful force in the universe is compound interest." The reverse is also true. If you lose principal, pay unnecessary costs or spend lavishly, rather than save, the lost return on those dollars compounds over time. I realize we have said this repeatedly throughout the book. That is intentional. If you learn nothing else from this book, learn to be cost conscious and cost sensitive.

The way the system is structured, the customer is likely to make less if the broker makes more. Customers should always be aware of that fact and, therefore, be as cost conscious as possible.

What if the system were structured so that the broker's earnings increased only if the client's portfolio performance increased? This would never happen, because that would mean the broker was taking market risk. The brokerage firm would never do that. Instead, they prefer to get their money, regardless of what happens to the customer, and to shift all market risk to the customer. From a monetary stand point, the brokerage firm has no incentive whatsoever, in most instances, to have the client post a profitable portfolio performance.

16. Don't attempt to practice market timing.

If the experts, as a group, consistently get this wrong, don't think you can outsmart them and be a successful market timer. They have access to more, and better, information and still are wrong more often than right.

17. Don't invest in limited partnerships.

There is almost never a good reason for the average investor to own a limited partnership. The only sensible reason is to invest in something you think would be fun or entertaining. The fees are excessive. The chances of success do not warrant the risks. These are often the investment choice of "advisors" who participate in commissions with originators. These, like many Wall Street products, are made for <u>selling</u>, not for <u>buying</u>. If you can't resist the temptation then refer back to #6.

18. Beware of success stories.

Hot tips from golf partners; investment advice from your brother-in-law. The sources of these stories are endless. The storytellers usually emphasize the positive and forget or ignore the negative. In some cases, they themselves may not even be aware of what the negatives are. Politely wish them well and ignore their "advice."

19. Understand the brutal math of the market.

If you invest $100,000 and lose half the money, you have lost 50%. To recoup the losses you then have to get a 100% return on the $50,000 you have left just to break even. Protect your principal with ferocious tenacity. Once gone, it is hard to replace.

20. Maximize tax benefits.

Here you need the advice of your accountant or your impartial advisor. Brokers are notorious for ignoring and/or not understanding the tax ramifications of the investments they <u>sell</u> you. This is especially true of mutual funds. Do not rely on your broker as a reliable source for this information.

21. Don't overvalue tax deductions.

Products are often sold because they involve a "tax deduction." A loss is a loss and a deduction does not recover the underlying loss. When you see banks post signs saying that they <u>BORROW</u> money, then you'll know that selling tax deductible investment strategies may have merit. However, don't hold your breath. Remember that any "tax-shelter" is, at best, a tax deferral, not a tax eliminator. Balance the cost and risk against the value of the "deferral."

22. Don't become a stock picker, or rely on someone who claims to have that ability.

Trying to pick winners in the stock market is like thinking you can be a successful market timer. If you must, use a portion of the 10 - 15 % (maximum) allocation for such whims but call it what it is, a gamble, not an investment.

23. Understand the impact of leverage and avoid its pitfalls.

Brokers are often guilty of trumpeting inflated returns that are the result of leverage. Don't be fooled. Leverage is a double edged sword. The high up-side returns can turn into devastating losses that can, in a flash, wipe out an entire portfolio. We've worked with many investors who failed to fully understand the risks of leverage and the use of margin. The results were, in many instances, devastating.

24. Beware of affinity fraud.

Brokers will use whatever method or device that works to gain the confidence and trust of prospective clients. The authors regularly hear the refrain of, "I met the broker in church. She seemed like such a nice person." We hate to turn readers into cynical skeptics but history tells us to be aware, and careful, of those who seek your trust and business based on common experiences or background. When seeking a doctor or dentist, you want the best professional you can find. Take the same approach in the financial arena. The friend of a friend isn't always a friend to you.

25. Take seriously your portfolio rebalancing.

Circumstances change. Some markets and products perform better than others. You should evaluate, adjust and rebalance your asset allocations at least annually, and preferably, on a quarterly basis.

26. Don't invest in hedge funds.

But wait, you say, aren't hedge funds the secret road to wealth? Not quite. It is, again, largely about fees and costs. The typical hedge fund charges a fee of 2% of assets and an incentive fee that is usually no less than 20% of the gains. Successes are touted. Failures are quietly boarded up and eliminated from average return calculations. The lack of any meaningful regulatory oversight increases the chances of negligence or outright fraud. Despite all the hoopla and the glorification of the few celebrity managers, the hedge fund industry, as a whole, underperforms market indexes. You won't hear that on CNBC.

27. If you do have an account with a brokerage firm, review and update the account opening documents regularly.

These documents are often used by the brokerage firms to deceive investors and are used against investors if a dispute occurs. Never inflate your net worth. Be totally truthful. You don't want to be the victim of a dishonest broker and then have the firm defend its actions by showing that you were less-than candid in the documents you signed.

Be equally careful in selecting your investment objectives. Most firms will ask you to list, in order of preference, your investment objectives. Typically, the choices are: income, growth, conservative or capital preservation, tax consequences, and speculation. Some firms omit the conservative or capital preservation option. This leaves you with no option for anything that, in the event of a dispute, would be considered less than "aggressive." Be demanding. Don't accept such an outrageous documentation of your investment "wishes, wants and desires."

Under the terms of FINRA Rule 2111 a broker may not recommend a security to a customer unless there's a reasonable basis for believing that the recommendation is suitable for that customer in light of the customer's financial situation and investment objectives.

Given many of the complex structured finance products being sold by broker dealers today, making a reasonable basis evaluation is more difficult and more important. We have encountered very few representatives who fully understand inferior tranches of collateralized debt obligations, particularly with the many nuances and subtleties embedded in those kinds of securities. That is just one example of the type of investments that contain huge commission credits for the sellers but have large embedded risks which have resulted in unmitigated disasters for many unsuspecting investors. When disputes arise, the brokers are often coached up by defense counsel and can present themselves as having a sufficient understanding of the product to meet the requirement of the rule. This is, in a vast majority of instances, after-the-fact training and a typical measure of closing the barn door long after the horses have escaped.

It is virtually impossible to suggest, with any degree of credibility, that the complex structured product investments are anything but speculative. Most investors do not have speculative checked as one of their investment objectives. Broker dealers try to justify these complex products as being suitable on the basis that they represent growth or income or that the investors fully understood the risk and did not deem them to be speculative.

We have seen many instances where the security sold to retail investors had below investment grade ratings. By the definitions used by the rating agencies "below investment grade" means the securities are speculative. Broker dealers generally have defended claims by pointing out that suitability is to be determined at the time of sale and not at any point thereafter. The new FINRA Rule 2111 requires the firm to extend the suitability analysis to include any investment strategy involving "an explicit recommendation to hold a security or securities."

This has far reaching impact because it means that the broker could well be liable if a recommendation to hold is made without the broker dealer having done sufficient analysis to determine the suitability of holding that investment under current conditions. It is important for a client to always keep a broker dealer informed as to changes in the investor's financial situation or

[208]

investment objectives due to educational needs of children or retirement expectations. The broker has an obligation to inquire about these but will, generally, testify in any dispute that inquiries were made and no appropriate responses were ever forthcoming. The inquiry may often take the form of a letter asking if there are any changes in status or objectives. Investors ignore these letters at their peril and often find them thrown in their face during arbitration.

28. Never buy securities on margin.

It can be an enormously risky venture for individual investors to buy securities on margin. All an investor needs to know about margin is just to never use it.

Brokerage firms are required to provide a Margin Disclosure Statement (FINRA Rule 2264) to customers before the customers are allowed to buy securities on margin. Unfortunately, the document is often accompanied by many verbal disclaimers and assurances that "the regulators require us to give you this."

A careful reading of the Margin Disclosure Statement should discourage all but committed gamblers from actively trading on margin:

2264. Margin Disclosure Statement
(a) No member shall open a margin account, as specified in Regulation T of the Board of Governors of the Federal Reserve System, for or on behalf of a non-institutional customer, unless, prior to or at the time of opening the account, the member has furnished to the customer, individually, in paper or electronic form, and in a separate document (or contained by itself on a separate page as part of another document), the margin disclosure statement specified in this paragraph (a). In addition, any member that permits non-institutional customers either to open accounts online or to engage in transactions in securities online must post such margin

disclosure statement on the member's Web site in a clear and conspicuous manner.

Margin Disclosure Statement

Your brokerage firm is furnishing this document to you to provide some basic facts about purchasing securities on margin, and to alert you to the risks involved with trading securities in a margin account. Before trading stocks in a margin account, you should carefully review the margin agreement provided by your firm. Consult your firm regarding any questions or concerns you may have with your margin accounts.

When you purchase securities, you may pay for the securities in full or you may borrow part of the purchase price from your brokerage firm. If you choose to borrow funds from your firm, you will open a margin account with the firm. The securities purchased are the firm's collateral for the loan to you. If the securities in your account decline in value, so does the value of the collateral supporting your loan, and, as a result, the firm can take action, such as issue a margin call and/or sell securities or other assets in any of your accounts held with the member, in order to maintain the required equity in the account.

It is important that you fully understand the risks involved in trading securities on margin. These risks include the following:

- You can lose more funds than you deposit in the margin account. A decline in the value of securities that are purchased on margin may require you to provide additional funds to the firm that has made the loan to avoid the forced sale of those securities or other securities or assets in your account(s).

- The firm can force the sale of securities or other assets in your account(s). If the equity in your account falls below the maintenance margin requirements, or the firm's higher "house" requirements, the firm can sell the securities or other assets in any of your accounts held at the firm to cover the margin deficiency. You also will be responsible for any short fall in the account after such a sale.

- <u>The firm can sell your securities or other assets without contacting you.</u> Some investors mistakenly believe that a firm must contact them for a margin call to be valid, and that the firm cannot liquidate securities or other assets in their accounts to meet the call unless the firm has contacted them first. This is not the case. Most firms will attempt to notify their customers of margin calls, but they are not required to do so. However, even if a firm has contacted a customer and provided a specific date by which the customer can meet a margin call, the firm can still take necessary steps to protect its financial interests, including immediately selling the securities without notice to the customer.

- <u>You are not entitled to choose which securities or other assets in your account(s) are liquidated or sold to meet a margin call.</u> Because the securities are collateral for the margin loan, the firm has the right to decide which security to sell in order to protect its interests.

- <u>The firm can increase its "house" maintenance margin requirements at any time and is not required to provide you advance written notice.</u> These changes in firm policy often take effect immediately and may result in the issuance of a maintenance margin call. Your failure to satisfy the call may cause the member to liquidate or sell securities in your account(s).

- <u>You are not entitled to an extension of time on a margin call.</u> While an extension of time to meet margin requirements may be available to

customers under certain conditions, a customer
does not have a right to the extension.

If you wouldn't borrow against the equity in your home to
trade securities, you should not borrow against the equity in your
investment portfolio to buy more securities.

29. Avoid "alternative" investments.

Lower commissions on many products and reduced yields on
fixed income investments have combined to cause brokerage firms
to push investors into "alternative" investments. These types of
investments take many forms but, generally, share several
characteristics: high fees, leverage, excessive risks, support from
internally generated analyses that emphasize upside potential and
downplay risks. The rewards seldom outweigh the risks. Avoid them.

30. Never borrow against the value of your home to make investments.

A March 2004 NASD alert said it best: NASD is issuing this
alert because we are concerned that investors who must rely on
investment returns to make their mortgage payments could end up
defaulting on their home loans if their investments decline and they
are unable to meet their monthly mortgage payments. In short,
investors who bet the ranch could lose it. In December 2004 in
NTM 04-89 the NASD expanded on these concerns:

> The rapid increase in home prices over the past
> several years, in combination with refinancing
> activity by homeowners, has lead to increasing
> investment activity by homeowners with equity
> from their homes. This Notice reminds members
> that recommending liquefying home equity to
> purchase securities may not be suitable for all
> investors and that members and their associated
> persons should perform a careful analysis to
> determine whether liquefying home equity is a
> suitable strategy for an investor. In addition,
> members should ensure that all communications
> with the public addressing a strategy of liquefying
> home equity are fair and balanced, and accurately

depict the risks of investing with liquefied home equity. Finally, members should consider whether to employ heightened scrutiny of accounts that they know, or have reason to know, are funded with liquefied home equity.

31. Don't trade commodities.

We have been approached by literally hundreds of "investors" who have suffered losses in commodity trading accounts. It is a FACT that we have never seen, or known, a <u>single</u> participant who was a customer of a commodities broker who ended the relationship with more money than they started with. Commodities trading accounts are the ultimate sucker's game. Don't become a victim.

32. Don't become a day trader.

There are television ads galore selling systems and encouraging day trading. The success stories are often fictional and even those that are true are a minuscule minority. Don't fall prey to the temptations of easy money. Generally, it is more likely to be an easy road to losses.

33. Don't buy shares in a fund which has substantial holdings of products you would not buy as free standing investments.

We see many investors who have told a broker they don't want to own "junk bonds" but are sold shares in junk bond funds. They are told that the holdings represent diversification and, thus, reduce the risk. To some extent this is true, but often these kinds of securities are highly correlated. When that market segment takes a precipitous drop, the fund ends up a big loser.

34. Beware switching holdings within an account which generates commissions.

This is a widespread practice, regularly engaged in by many Wall Street firms. It occurs most often with mutual funds but is also done in individual holdings of stocks and bonds.

Brokers tout switching from one holding into another holding with better prospects for gain or higher yields.

There is typically no charge for switching within a family of no-load mutual funds. However, a charge will usually have to be paid when switching from one load fund to another or when switching from one family of funds to another.

Get a full explanation of any switching, swap, trade or transaction your broker recommends. Make sure you know the benefits, risks and costs before agreeing to such a change.

35. Never sign agreements to open an account or have someone manage your money during the first meeting.

Be cautious. Take notes. Seek references. Follow up and get second or multiple opinions on what you are being told. There is great merit in the 24-48 hour rule. Think it over. Consider the negatives. Don't rush, or allow yourself to be rushed, into such an important decision. We find that next to life, health, family and in some cases faith, money is the next most important thing to many individuals. Don't make decisions casually or on a whim. Bad financial decisions will almost always impact an individual's ability to enjoy the most meaningful areas of their life.

36. Beware of preferred stock.

This is a great quote from Allan Roth, a Certified Financial Planner, in an article he wrote for the AARP magazine:

> Bad advice is epidemic in my industry, and it doesn't come only from villainous fraudsters such as Madoff. It also comes from pleasant and pathetic folks who are merely responding predictably to my industry's perverse incentives and self-serving ethical standards.

Sometimes, the biggest threats to trusting investors can be from their friends and those that truly care about them. A person can be well meaning and still rip you off.

[214]

Preferred stocks are a classic example of products sold by, often times, well meaning brokers who did not understand the product or the risks embedded in them. They compare the products to bonds; sell them as fixed income instruments and often imply that the products are as "safe" as bonds. Investors are also told that preferred stock is more secure than common stock and is therefore, "safer." The fact is preferred stock is <u>SOLD</u> by broker dealers, primarily, because it is a high commission item.

Investors should be aware of additional facts that are seldom brought up in sales presentations encouraging the purchase of preferred stocks:
   a) The maturity dates are extremely long in almost every issue.
   b) If a company issues preferred stocks, it probably means they are limited in the ability to issue bonds or sell more common stock.
   c) In most instances, if a company fails, the common stock <u>AND</u> the preferred stock become virtually worthless.

Beware. In the real world of preferred stocks, the negatives generally outweigh the positives.

37. Don't ratify your broker's errors.
Brokers, and especially their managers and supervisors, are highly skilled at presenting and selling products. They are equally skilled at deflecting blame back onto a customer when things have gone wrong. Do not be lured into making verbal or written admissions or accepting blame for bad advice provided by the broker or the brokerage firm.

Brokerage firms are masters of manipulating conversations and statements to their advantage and to the detriment of customers. Don't become a victim of this kind of manipulation.

38. Do not ignore ETFs.

ETFs (Exchange Traded Funds) are being used by a growing number of investors as an alternative to mutual funds. From early 2011 to early 2012, investors increased equity based ETF holdings by $74.2 Billion, while withdrawing $100.6 Billion from equity based mutual funds. ETFs are designed to be less costly than mutual funds and to provide a market return. An ETF is designed to follow the movement of a specific market, be it stocks, bonds, commodities, gold or even a specific industry.

ETFs were created to make it easier to purchase a basket of stocks reflecting the overall performance of a particular market. In suggesting that investors take advantage of the opportunities afforded by ETFs, we are recommending passive ETFs, not those that are actively managed. Generally, the goal of an ETF is to emulate an underlying index.

In addition to reflecting the actual performance, of whatever market you choose, ETFs offer numerous other advantages. They have substantial tax advantages, liquidity, are a reasonably simple product to understand, and offer minimal transaction costs.

TD Ameritrade offers advantages over other discount brokers, as a source for ETFs as shown on one of their marketing pieces:

The Most Commission-Free ETFs*		How many commission-free ETFs available?	From what ETF issuers?	Commission-free ETFs selected by an unbiased third-party?
Straightforward Pricing	TD Ameritrade	100+	iShares, Powershares, SPDR*, Vanguard and more	Yes Selected by Morningstar Associates MORNINGSTAR
Powerful, Easy-to-Use Trading Tools	Schwab	15	Schwab	No
Experienced Help 24/7	Fidelity	30	iShares	No
	Vanguard	49	Vanguard	No
Free Independent Research	E-Trade	93	Deutsche, WisdomTree, Global X	No
	Scottrade	15	FocusShares	No

A good summary on ETFs is set out on the SEC website:

Most ETFs seek to achieve the same return as a particular market index. That type of ETF is similar to an index fund in that it will primarily invest in the securities of companies that are included in a selected market index. An ETF will invest in either all of the securities or a representative sample of the securities included in the index. For example, one type of ETF, known as Spiders or SPDRs, invests in all of the stocks contained in the S&P 500 Composite Stock Price Index. Other types of ETFs include leveraged or inverse ETFs, which are ETFs that seek to achieve a daily return that is a multiple, or an inverse multiple, of the daily return of a securities index. An important characteristic of these ETFs is that they seek to achieve their stated objectives on a daily basis, and their performance over longer periods of time can differ significantly from the multiple, or inverse multiple, of the index performance over those longer periods of time. ETFs also include actively managed ETFs that pursue active management strategies and publish their portfolio holdings on a daily basis.

Additional background information is provided by Investopedia:

Because it trades like a stock, an ETF does not have its net asset value (NAV) calculated every day like a mutual fund does.

By owning an ETF, you get the diversification of an index fund as well as the ability to sell short, buy on margin and purchase as little as one share. Another advantage is that the expense ratios for most ETFs are lower than those of the average mutual fund. When buying and selling ETFs, you have to pay the same commission to your broker that you'd pay on any regular order.

There are some ETF limitations and potential problems that investors should be aware of. For instance, there are a large number of ETF products available for U.S. markets but somewhat fewer options in foreign markets.

In addition, investors should avoid leveraged ETFs. Due to daily resets the leveraged ETFs are exposed, over time, to value delay. There can be, and often are, wide variances in ETF fees. As mentioned elsewhere, this is especially true when dealing with major Wall Street firms.

Some ETFs have low trading volumes, which can lead to larger than normal bid-ask spreads, which can eat into returns.

Even given the cautionary issues with ETFs, in considering passive investment alternatives, investors should look beyond mutual funds and consider the advantages of ETFs.

39. Don't automatically blame yourself for your investment losses.

If you make all of your investment decisions, then you are responsible for the results you get. However, if you use a broker and rely on their advice, <u>DO NOT BLAME YOURSELF</u> for what happens in your account.

Brokerage firms spend millions of dollars every year to convince prospective customers that they can provide everything necessary for a secure financial future. Brokers are quick to take full credit for upward swings in the market. However, they want no part of any blame for anything negative that happens in your account. They are equally quick to blame the market for any and all losses.

If you have a mechanic, a plumber or any other type of service provider you don't blame yourself for their bad advice or work performance. Yet, clients constantly accept blame heaped on them by their "trusted financial advisors" or take responsibility for the broker's failings. Don't ever be enticed into making statements to your broker blaming yourself for negative events in your portfolio.

You may well hear those words quoted back to you in an arbitration hearing.

40. Evaluate Potential Investment Advisors

An investor needs to first decide the kind of investment advisor they want to have. We have suggested that independent, fee based advisors offer the best route to success. We are aware that some investors will continue to work with major brokerage firms. The advice set out below is primarily intended to help those investors who choose to work with full service registered investment brokerage firms. However, many of the suggestions will also be helpful to those seeking advice, or counsel, from other types of investment professionals.

Before hiring an investment professional, it is wise to investigate the broker and the brokerage firm. The Internet provides a convenient means for obtaining important background information on all registered representatives, brokerage firms and investment advisors. Below is a checklist for finding an appropriate investment professional:

- ✓ Determine the level of service desired. Some brokerage firms provide recommendations, investment advice, and research support, while others may not. The fees charged may differ depending upon what services are provided by the firm.

- ✓ Get names of professionals from friends, neighbors, family or business colleagues.

- ✓ Meet with several professionals. Meet them face-to-face in their offices, if possible. Ask them about their:

    - Areas of specialization
    - Professional designations
    - Registrations or licenses
    - Education
    - Work history

- Investment experience
- Products and services
- Disciplinary history

✓ Understand how the firm or individual will be paid. Investment professionals are typically paid in one of the following ways:

- An hourly fee
- A flat fee
- A commission on the investment products they sell
- A percentage of the value of the assets they manage
- A combination of fees and commissions.

✓ Ask whether they receive any additional compensation or financial incentives based on the products they sell. Sometimes, investments professionals and their firms receive additional compensation for selling a particular mutual fund or other investment product.

✓ Ask if the firm is a member of the Securities Investor Protection Corporation (SIPC). SIPC provides limited customer protection if a firm becomes insolvent. Ask if the firm has other insurance that provides coverage beyond the SIPC limit. SIPC does not insure against losses attributable to a decline in the market value of your securities.

✓ Make sure that the investment professionals and their firms are properly registered with FINRA, the U.S. Securities and Exchange Commission and/or a state insurance or securities regulator. Most investment professionals need to register as investment advisors, investment advisor representatives or brokers (registered representatives). Others may only be licensed to sell insurance.

✓ Check out the disciplinary history of any brokerage firm and sales representative through FINRA BrokerCheck or by calling 1-800-289-9999.

FINRA BrokerCheck is a free and convenient tool to help investors examine the professional background of current and former FINRA-registered brokerage firms and brokers as well as investment advisor firms and representatives.

BrokerCheck provides information on disciplinary actions taken by securities regulators and criminal authorities and also includes specific information on investor complaints.

The information about brokers and brokerage firms made available through BrokerCheck is obtained from the Central Registration Depository (CRD®)[11].

Resources available to investors from FINRA BrokerCheck include:

❖ Centralized access to licensing and registration information on current and former brokers and brokerage firms, investment advisor representatives and investment advisor firms;

❖ The ability to search for, and locate, a financial services professional based on main office and branch locations, and the ability to conduct ZIP code radius searches for brokerage firms; and

❖ Access to expanded educational content available on BrokerCheck, including

---

[11] Central Registration Depository (CRD) – An online computerized system in which FINRA maintains the employment, qualification and disciplinary histories of more than 650,000 securities industry professionals and more than 5,000 brokerage firms that deal with the public.

explanations of commonly used terms throughout the BrokerCheck system.

✓ Investors should also check with state regulators. The NASAA provides contact information for individual state securities regulators. The state regulator's office will also have a report on all brokers, which may include additional information on a registered representative or brokerage firm. Contact NASAA through its website www.nasaa.org for more information on each state's securities commission.

For the most part, the above advice is offered to those investors who decide they want to deal with a broker dealer registered with FINRA. For many investors, a better choice may be to select an independent, fee based advisor.

41. Write to your Congressional representatives.

The Wall Street lobbyists are comparable in power to the pharmaceutical, insurance, and oil industries. The campaign dollars that go to elected officials from Wall Street are staggering. Other indirect perks add additional millions, flowing from Wall Street to elected representatives.

Fight back! Write to elected officials, whether from your own district or elsewhere. Urge the restoration of Glass-Steagall. This would eliminate risky securities trading by banking institutions relying on insured deposits.

Share the stories from this book, or your own experiences, about Wall Street negligence, greed and fraud. Demand that investors be given an option of pursuing claims in court or through arbitration.

Organize group letter writing campaigns through pensions and other organizations to which you belong.

Chapter 12
Become a FINRA Arbitrator

There has been an ongoing chorus of complaints about the lack of impartiality on the part of FINRA arbitrators. No matter how horrific the abuse, or how compelling a claim may be, investors have little chance of fully recovering lost funds if forced before a biased panel which favors industry arguments and positions.

It is as critical to have impartial arbitrators hear a case as it is to have impartial jurors sitting in judgment of their peers in a courtroom. Wall Street firms expend a lot of time, energy and money recruiting arbitrators favorable to their positions. One of the authors was told by the partner of a major law firm which represents several Wall Street firms that he was pressured to recruit arbitrators. He indicated that he was told by one of his clients to "find time to recruit a few favorably inclined arbitrators," or the firm could easily find another lawyer.

Investors need to fight back. They need to aggressively seek (and become) truly impartial arbitrators who can hear arbitration claims with an open mind. The process of becoming an arbitrator is not easy. In order to sit as a juror, you don't have to meet any qualifications other than to demonstrate impartiality. FINRA insists that their arbitrators be first screened, and then, if found to be "qualified," they must then be "trained."

There are no such "qualifying" or "training" requirements for jury members. FINRA justifies this process because the industry and the products sold by the member firms are complex and require specific training to be able to understand the case presentations. The contradictory nature of this thinking is underscored by the fact that, in the vast majority of cases, brokerage firms defend the case by claiming that the wronged consumer was a "sophisticated investor" and fully understood the risks of the complex product being sold to them.

It is frustrating to sit in a hearing and have a broker with many years of experience in the industry be exposed as having little or no knowledge of a particular product he had been selling. However, in the same hearing, the brokerage firm will brand a full time surgeon with the label of "sophisticated investor" because he has "been investing in stocks for 20 years." As one doctor client put it, "After sitting through this hearing, I assume what they want me to do is stop seeing patients and spend all of my time overseeing my investments. I thought that's what I hired them to do!" The idea that a full-time brain surgeon can be a part-time financial expert is almost as absurd as having the full-time broker be a medical expert in his spare time. Yet, this argument is made successfully, time after time, before the FINRA "screened," "qualified" and "trained" arbitrators.

The rest of this chapter is devoted to how you, the reader, can become an arbitrator and help balance the scales of financial justice. We urge you to take the step, if it is possible in your personal life, to actively recruit scores of others willing to offer themselves for public service to protect investors, pensioners and retirees. FINRA arbitrators have the power to make Wall Street accountable.

Given the make-up of most current FINRA panels, the brokerage firms, based on a long history, go into a hearing knowing that, even if a finding is rendered in favor of the Claimant, a small percentage of the losses will be awarded. The most helpful thing an investor can do to help not only themselves, but all investors, is to become a FINRA Arbitrator. FINRA Dispute Resolution has a serious deficit of non-biased arbitrators. There is no organized effort on the part of any investor group to recruit arbitrators.

The authors of this book were inspired to continue the process of recruiting arbitrators by a recent story. One of the authors was approached by an individual who had recently been recruited to become an arbitrator. Her comments were both revealing and shocking, but sadly, not at all surprising.

She first expressed her thanks for help in becoming an arbitrator. She then said:

> "I just finished my FINRA training and am officially an arbitrator. I see, now, why you work so hard to recruit arbitrators and try to level the playing field. In the group of new recruits I was part of, I frankly cannot imagine a single one of them ever being sympathetic toward the plight of an investor. They all commented that the investors had a duty to monitor their accounts closely and to order the broker to stop any activity which was detrimental to their financial interest. I tried to explain to them that their position was not a standard that would be applied in any other field. I also mentioned that most investors wouldn't know they were being abused until well after the fact. However, I didn't seem to make any progress in denting their solidly entrenched feelings."

In truth, this kind of thinking would not be normal or acceptable in any other field or profession. Patients would not be held liable for failing to prevent a surgical mistake. Clients would not be held responsible for failing to remind an attorney to avoid having the statute of limitations expire prior to the filing of a cause of action.

Imagine a lawsuit against a plumber in which the defense is that the pipes belong to the homeowner and it is, therefore, the homeowner's responsibility to protect themselves from any mistakes the plumber might make. The same homeowner would not be held liable for failing to tell the roofer how to prevent future leaks. Absurd examples you say? Indeed, the examples are absurd because no one would ever suggest that such responsibilities would fall to users, customers or clients. Yet, in the field of arbitration, given the kinds of arbitrators so aggressively recruited by the securities industry, this kind of thinking sadly represents the norm, not the exception.

Some background on the FINRA arbitration process is necessary in order to paint an accurate picture of exactly why it is so important to have more (a lot more) public arbitrators.

Background

As previously mentioned, all disputes between investors and their securities firms, or broker dealers, are required to be tried before a FINRA arbitration panel. Every investor, when opening an account, waives their right to have any potential dispute heard in court and submits themselves to the FINRA Dispute Resolution arbitration forum.

As pointed out earlier, FINRA is a securities industry trade organization that is largely funded by its members, who are all registered securities dealers.

For investor cases where the amount in controversy exceeds $100,000, FINRA assembles a panel of three arbitrators. There are some distinctions in the types of FINRA arbitrators who hear investor dispute cases. First, there are public arbitrators. These individuals are not required to have prior knowledge of the securities industry, but have been pre-approved by FINRA and have gone through the training required by FINRA. Second, there are Chair-qualified arbitrators. These arbitrators must be public arbitrators who have demonstrated enough experience to serve as the Chairperson of a Panel during the arbitration process. Many of the Chair-qualified arbitrators are attorneys, but not all.

The third category is that of the non-public arbitrator (often referred to as an "industry" arbitrator). Non-public arbitrators, by definition, have an extensive securities industry background. They work or have worked directly for a FINRA member.

Interestingly, registered financial advisors (RIAs) are not allowed to be FINRA arbitrators. This is the height of hypocrisy. An RIA is defined by The Investment Advisors Act of 1940 as a "person or firm that, for compensation, is engaged in the act of providing advice, making recommendations, issuing reports or furnishing analyses on securities, either directly or through publications." Investment advisors have a fiduciary duty to their clients, which means that they have a fundamental obligation to provide suitable investment advice and always act in the clients' best interests.

RIAs are also called "money managers" or "financial planners." RIAs are not FINRA members, although FINRA is now seeking authority to regulate RIAs. RIAs have different licensing requirements, different standards of duty, and do not work for FINRA members. They are regulated by the states and by the SEC, but not FINRA (at least not yet). They do provide financial advice to investors and obviously have knowledge of the industry, so logic would dictate that they would be ideal candidates for the non-public arbitrator positions. However, this is not the case. Why not?

RIAs and registered representatives are often at odds with one another. Time and again it is the RIA who first notices the wrongdoing of a broker when the customer switches from a registered broker dealer to an RIA. RIAs are held to a higher standard of fiduciary duty (by federal regulators) than registered brokers, but they are not securities salespeople.

RIAs are often paid hourly or on a fee basis, but they are generally not paid on commission, as is usually the case with a registered FINRA member. If FINRA sincerely wants arbitrators who understand the industry and the products sold by broker dealers, then RIAs would seem to be much in demand. For whatever reasons, however, despite their clear-cut appropriate credentials, RIAs are not allowed to serve as even non-public arbitrators for FINRA arbitration. As an investor, this practice by FINRA should be a red flag as to what investors face when they attempt to go against the Wall Street firms in their own forum.

For years, until protest from investor groups were successful in abolishing the practice, FINRA panels, in cases brought by investors, required the inclusion of two public arbitrators and one industry arbitrator. The parties can still agree to have an industry arbitrator but it is no longer a requirement. The inclusion of an industry arbitrator is now determined by the investor. The practice of the mandatory inclusion of an industry arbitrator on every panel was very controversial due to the obvious bias, or at least the appearance of bias, of the non-public arbitrator. The professed purpose of an industry arbitrator was to provide the arbitration panel with expert knowledge of the industry. In practice, however, to provide a comparison, it was like being forced to have a medical malpractice case heard by the American Medical Association rather than by a jury, and at least one of three panelists deciding the case being a doctor.

Investors can now use the new panel selection method which is known as the Optional All Public Panel rule, or the previous panel selection method which is the Majority Public Panel rule. Customers (investors) choose the panel selection method; the brokerage firms do not have a vote on the method selected. The All Public Panel option includes all customer cases (whether the customer is a claimant or a respondent). FINRA is to be applauded for making this change, although it clearly came about as a result of public pressure, not because FINRA, without pressure, initiated the change. The largest and most effective pressure was put forth by the Public Investors Arbitration Bar Association (PIABA), an organization of securities arbitration attorneys, which lobbied for years to eliminate the industry arbitrator.

The option for the all public arbitration panel is great news for investors, but the new rule has also created increased demand for public arbitrators. Due to the demand for public arbitrators, it is even more important for individuals to come forward and become an arbitrator. As of May 16, 2012, there were 3,572 public arbitrators and 2,878 non-public arbitrators.

The available arbitrator pool, which was already in need of additional public arbitrators, is now in serious need of additional candidates due to the elimination of the non-public arbitrators from the pools for Optional All Public panels. Every investor who becomes an arbitrator takes a giant step toward more transparency in the securities industry and more accountability for the brokerage firms.

The general lack of public arbitrators is not the only problem. Within the available "public" arbitrator pools sit many seasoned, veteran arbitrators who are still not truly impartial. Many of the arbitrators who serve on cases thoroughly enjoy being an arbitrator and, as such, do what they believe is necessary to serve as often as possible on as many cases as possible. Many arbitrators are retirees who rely on the extra income. Arbitrators are paid substantially more than jurors, earning $200 to $400 a day (or more) for their service.

The parties to FINRA arbitration select the arbitrators from a "random" list of qualified arbitrators provided by FINRA. The parties are supplied with a disclosure report (information sheet) for each potential panelist. This report lists the arbitrator's education, employment history, conflicts of interest, and access to the outcome of every case in arbitration they have previously decided. Each party has the opportunity to rank the potential panelists from each category (Chair, Public and Non-Public) in order of preference. The parties may also disqualify or strike up to four arbitrators on each list. The investor party may now strike every non-public or industry arbitrator, but they are offered the opportunity to rank any of them if they choose to do so.

The problem for investors is that the brokerage firms are always the repeat customers in arbitration. Investors are rarely (and thankfully) involved in more than one FINRA arbitration in a lifetime. This places investors, again, at a huge disadvantage. Since the brokerage firms find themselves involved in multiple arbitrations at any given time, they are routinely selecting arbitrators. The brokerage firms will select the arbitrators who demonstrate records that are favorable to the industry, thus, increasing their odds of victory at every arbitration hearing. This practice also influences the pre-hearing settlements, since they are always negotiated on the basis of the likely outcome at arbitration.

[230]

If the pool of arbitrators can be balanced out with more impartial arbitrators, investor disputes are likely to achieve a much more favorable percentage of awards for investors. For investors to win less than half of the cases taken to a hearing is shocking. It would suggest that investors and their legal representatives are bringing many claims that lack merit. Given the pressure placed on claimants, and that their attorneys almost always work on a contingency basis, it defies common sense to suggest that false claims would be regularly brought before FINRA panels.

Requirements for Becoming an Arbitrator

The requirements for becoming an arbitrator are challenging, but not overwhelming. FINRA requires five years of full-time, paid business or professional experience (inside or outside of the securities industry), and at least two years of college-level credits. This education requirement would eliminate many self-made and or self-educated individuals who would NOT be stricken from the jury pool for the courts. The FINRA arbitration program seeks arbitrators from varied backgrounds. FINRA arbitrators are not FINRA employees, but serve as independent contractors who serve at FINRA's discretion. We have actively recruited arbitrators from many walks of life.

The authors encourage those who are interested in becoming a FINRA arbitrator to take the first step by completing the application which can be found by going to the FINRA website at www.finra.org.

Do not let the length of the application be intimidating. Although the application may appear daunting, it is actually seeking only the following information:
- Biographical information (name, address, date of birth, etc.)
- Educational background
- Employment information, and
- Professional affiliations, if any.

The rest of the application is simply requesting disclosure information for determining conflicts of interest. For example, if an arbitrator has had a brokerage account at Morgan Stanley for 10 years, that arbitrator could be asked to recuse himself (remove himself from the Panel), or FINRA could remove the arbitrator upon a request from either party. That arbitrator would not be disqualified for a case against any firm where there are no ties, however. For someone who has employment experience with the securities industry, the questions will be familiar. For anyone who does not have considerable experience with the securities industry, most of the questions will not be applicable.

The application requires two letters of recommendation. These need not be lengthy. A sample letter, which was part of a successful application, is set out below:

FINRA Dispute Resolution
Department of Neutral Management
One Liberty Plaza
165 Broadway, 27th Floor
New York, NY 10006

Re: Arbitrator application of Robert E. Jones

To Whom It May Concern:

I am writing this letter in support of Mr. Robert E. Jones' application to serve as an arbitrator. I have known Mr. Jones for approximately 4 years through our mutual involvement in securities litigation. As a FINRA arbitrator and as one who has worked with attorneys who represent parties in numerous arbitration proceedings, I can say that Mr. Jones is well qualified to serve as an arbitrator, both as a matter of intellect and as a matter of temperament.

I know Mr. Jones to be fair, open minded, patient, and courteous. I have no doubt that he will be willing to consider all points of view and to give all decisions the time and deliberation that they deserve. In short, he has the character and fitness to serve as an arbitrator.

Sincerely,

Connie J. Becker
Paralegal
FINRA Arbitrator
#A55762

This sample letter can be used as a guide for anyone who would like to apply to be an arbitrator.

Required Basic Arbitrator Training
It is not necessary to have specific knowledge about the arbitration process, or the securities industry, prior to submitting an application to become an arbitrator. All required arbitrator training is provided by FINRA, free of charge, and is conveniently available online. FINRA has suspended all fees for arbitrator training indefinitely. Beware that FINRA may reinstate the fees at a later date.

Once FINRA approves the arbitrator candidate's application, the individual must complete the Basic Arbitrator Training Program to become eligible to serve on arbitration cases. The Basic Arbitrator Training Program covers the arbitration process and reviews the procedures that arbitrators must follow to successfully complete an arbitration case. Most candidates find this training to be interesting and beneficial as well as educational.

What Do Arbitrators Do?
Arbitrators hear all sides of the issues as presented by the parties, study the evidence, and then decide how to resolve the matter.

Arbitrators, as the sole decision makers on securities cases, wield significant power. Arbitrator decisions are final and binding within the FINRA Dispute Resolution process. The only way to overturn an arbitrator decision is to appeal to an appellate court. The appeal process offers only limited options and most awards appealed are upheld by the courts.

Where do the Arbitrations Take Place?

Arbitrations normally take place in the city where the investor (Claimant) lived at the time the dispute arose. FINRA has offices throughout the United States. If the investor does not live within a reasonable distance to a FINRA office, the hearings often take place in a local hotel conference room. Likewise, in most cases, the arbitrators are selected from the geographic area nearest to where the Claimant resides, which is normally where the hearing will take place.

All pre-hearing conferences take place over the telephone and are coordinated by FINRA. There is no need to travel prior to the final arbitration. In addition, the parties and each arbitrator are all involved in setting the hearing date. The dates for the hearing will be set for a time when the parties, every attorney, and every arbitrator is available. The arbitrations are usually planned at least six months in advance, so that fitting an arbitration hearing into one's schedule is convenient for everyone involved. Arbitrators can volunteer to make themselves available to travel to other cities based on FINRA's demand for arbitrators in certain areas. When arbitrators do travel, FINRA reimburses the costs of travel to the arbitrators.

Benefits of Being a FINRA Arbitrator

In addition to helping improve the arbitration process for all investors, there are other benefits to being a FINRA arbitrator. Arbitrators enjoy the benefits of added knowledge about the industry, which makes them more informed and successful investors. Arbitrators can take satisfaction in knowing they are adding a valuable service to an industry that is need of more fair-minded decision makers. While no one is getting rich as an arbitrator, the fees can provide supplemental income, especially for retirees.

Stressing the importance of becoming a FINRA arbitrator is a high priority to the authors. If any questions arise when reviewing the application to become an arbitrator, feel free to direct an e-mail to the authors for assistance.

www.dlsecuritieslaw.com
dledbetter@dlsecuritieslaw.com
cbecker@dlsecuritieslaw.com

The authors have been successfully recruiting arbitrators for many years and are aware that the process is not simple. They are willing to review applications and answer questions for anyone willing to take on the task of becoming a FINRA arbitrator.

Potential candidates can also seek help from PIABA at www.piaba.org or contact FINRA directly through www.finra.org.

As readers consider their own role in FINRA arbitration, it is hoped that the following excerpt from a commencement address, by author Michael Lewis,[12] to the 2012 Princeton University graduates will provide inspiration to anyone who is concerned about making a difference:

"Don't Eat Fortune's Cookie"

> "I called up my father. I told him I was going to quit this job that now promised me millions of dollars to write a book for an advance of 40 grand. There was a long pause on the other end of the line. "You might just want to think about that," he said.
>
> "Why?"

---

[12] Michael Lewis is the best-selling author of *Liar's Poker, Moneyball, The Blind Side, and Home Game.*

"Stay at Salomon Brothers 10 years, make your fortune, and then write your books," he said.

I didn't need to think about it. I knew what intellectual passion felt like — because I'd felt it here, at Princeton — and I wanted to feel it again. I was 26 years old. Had I waited until I was 36, I would never have done it. I would have forgotten the feeling."

***

The authors urge you to make a great public service to abused investors by becoming a FINRA arbitrator and recruiting other eligible friends and family members to join you.

So now you know what you are up against. You have learned that the primary goal of many brokers and all full-service brokerage firms is to get as much of your hard-earned money as possible. Against this harrowing background, we offer 41 suggestions on how to defend yourself, and your money, against the highly organized and well financed efforts of the brokerage firms claiming to be there to help you.

If you use the suggestions on this list it will be difficult for the brokerage industry predators to victimize you. A wise sage once shared with me a lesson that should guide your financial decision making:

Discipline by others is tyranny.
The only true freedom is self-discipline.

Use this list to guard your precious assets. Have the discipline necessary to protect yourself.

***

HORROR STORY

A retired teacher was sold a VRA by a representative of a Wall Street broker. As time went by, she suspected that the VRA was the wrong investment for her. It was so wrong, in fact, that after losing over $200,000 in two years she complained to the Wall Street broker. An internal investigation was supposedly undertaken and she was advised that the market went down and "things happen." According to the internal investigation, the firm itself and the representatives who sold the products had done nothing wrong.

After complaining to the SEC, NASD and the State Department of Securities with no success, she hired an attorney to bring an arbitration claim against the brokerage house involved in the sale of the VRAs. The securities arbitration process was initiated and three supposedly neutral, unbiased and non-conflicted arbitrators were chosen to hear the case.

Suddenly, within a few weeks before the securities arbitration hearing on this dispute was scheduled to take place, the parties were advised that one of the "chosen" arbitrators on the panel was being replaced by what is referred to as a "cram down" arbitrator. A short two page disclosure about the cram down arbitrator was sent to the parties. The disclosure contained little, or no, information which would address the cram down arbitrator's bias, ethics or conflicts with the case. At that point, settlement negotiations broke down with no explanation from the brokerage firm.

The arbitration started and was scheduled to last five days. The first day of arbitration was routine with one minor exception. The cram down arbitrator, who was also a member of the securities industry, and was, at the time, employed by a major brokerage house, asked some questions of the Claimant's first witness which reflected a thorough knowledge about the sale of VRAs.

In preparing for the second day of hearing, early that morning, co-counsel for the Claimant briefly discussed the questions asked the previous afternoon by the cram down industry arbitrator. A thorough investigation was initiated on the industry arbitrator. The investigation revealed something far more sinister than the innocuous disclosure provided by FINRA. The cram down industry arbitrator had actually been sued in a case with "eerily similar" facts and circumstances. In addition, the arbitrator had recently been fired by his brokerage house employer for conduct which was non-compliance related. The broker's CRD had not been properly updated and none of this information was provided to the Claimant's attorney prior to the arbitration. If these facts had been known to the Claimant when the cram down appeared on the scene, there would have been a successful "challenge for cause." The cram down arbitrator appeared biased, not neutral, and potentially conflicted in relation to the facts of the case.

Due to FINRA's failure to disclose pertinent and important information to the parties, the victim's case was being heard by an arbitrator who had been sued for the same facts and products for which the Claimant was suing the Respondents. Unless the cram down arbitrator could equal the ethics of an ancient philosopher, capable of setting aside personal bias in favor of another party, the former teacher was in trouble with this cram down hearing her case.

Here is a dirty little secret about securities arbitration. FINRA's failure to provide complete or meaningful information about proposed or cram down arbitrators to public customers is, at worst deceitful, and, at least negligent. Whether deceitful or negligent, the harm done to the investor is the same. Remember, the Claimant had no choice. She was required, by virtue of the account opening documents she signed, to pursue her claims before a FINRA arbitration panel. She cannot pursue a remedy in court and is dependent on the FINRA process to assume that a case is being heard by neutral and unbiased arbitrators.

In FINRA arbitrations, full disclosures about arbitrators, are often not provided. The problem becomes worse with "cram down" arbitrators who are "not chosen" by the parties as all other arbitrators, but are simply appointed.

The belated challenge, to the "cram down" arbitrator, resulted in the brokerage house agreeing to a settlement of the case for a substantial sum of money. This story has a happy ending but far too many similar stories do not.

***

The horror stories throughout this book all take place after the fact. Be prepared. Be defensive.

[238]

Appendix

Key Definitions

The following are key definitions of industry terms you may not have heard.

Accrued Interest
Interest deemed to be earned on a security but not yet paid to the investor.

Active Return
A return relative to a benchmark. If a portfolio's return is 8%, and the benchmark's return is 5%, then the portfolio's active return is 3%.

Alpha
Alpha measures the difference between a fund's actual results and the results that a statistically average fund having the same sensitivity to market movements in the same category would be expected to achieve.

Amortization
Liquidation of a debt through installment payments.

Annualized Gain
The percentage gain in a period multiplied by the number of periods in a year. If a stock appreciates 2% in one month, the annualized gain is 24%.

Average Life
On a mortgage security, the average life is the average time until a dollar of principal is repaid, weighted by the amount of each principal payment, based on prepayment assumptions.

Basis Point
One-hundredth (.01) of a percentage point. Yield changes and differences among bonds are stated in basis points.

Benchmark Index

An independently created and calculated security index having the closest correlation to an investment fund against which the manager's performance is regularly measured.

Beta

Beta is a measure of an investment's sensitivity to market movements. The beta of the entire stock market is 1.0. A security or portfolio with a beta of less than 1.0 is less volatile than the market. A security with a beta greater than 1.0 is more volatile. Therefore, a beta of 1.0 represents the volatility of the market for a given period of time. Typically, the S&P 500 is used as the benchmark index and proxy for "the market" against which individual stocks or mutual funds measure their beta.

Bond Equivalent Yield

An adjustment to a Collateralized Mortgage Obligation (CMO) yield which reflects its greater present value. It is created because CMOs pay monthly or quarterly interest, unlike most types of bonds, which pay interest semiannually.

Correlation (R-Squared)

A measurement of how closely a portfolio's performance compares with the performance of a benchmark index, such as the S&P 500.

Cost-Equity Ratio

Sometimes called the "break-even" ratio; cost-equity indicates what portion of the portfolio's value is being spent on transaction costs and margin interest. It also shows how much a portfolio would have to generate in investment returns in order to cover the costs.

Current Face

The current remaining principal on a mortgage security. Current face is computed by multiplying the original face value of the security by the current principal balance factor.

Diversification

The process by which an investor can eliminate, or reduce, certain risks by spreading investments across asset classes and among many securities within each asset class.

Downside Capture Ratio

A measure of an investment's performance in down markets relative to the market itself. A value of 90% suggests the investment's loss is only nine-tenths of the market's loss.

Duration

A term used in fixed interest markets, reflecting a fund's sensitivity to interest rate changes. Duration measures the average time required to receive all payments from a security, principal as well as interest, taking into account its eventual maturity and the frequency and amount of the income payments. The longer a fund's duration, the greater its sensitivity to long-term interest rate movements.

Earnings Per Share

The amount of profit of an enterprise attributable to each ordinary share.

Expungement

The process of removing information from a broker's record in the Central Registration Depository (CRD®) System is called "expungement." Brokerage firms must submit a disclosure report when a broker is the "subject of" allegations of sales practice violations made in arbitration claims or civil lawsuits, but is not a named party to the arbitration or lawsuit. Once reported, this information is recorded on the broker's record in the CRD® System and becomes available to the public upon request through FINRA's BrokerCheck program.

Brokers may seek to have a reference to allegations or to involvement in an arbitration, removed from their CRD® System records.

Extension Risk

The risk that rising interest rates may slow the anticipated prepayment speeds, causing investors to find their principal committed longer than they expected.

Face Value

The principal amount of a security at par value, which is the amount that will be paid at maturity.

Factor

A decimal value reflecting the proportion of the outstanding principal balance of a mortgage security, which changes over time, in relation to its original principal value.

Fiduciary

An individual, or organization, responsible for managing assets in the best interest of the beneficiary and never for personal gain.

Financial Suicide

An investor is said to be committing financial suicide if he or she engages in trading that is contrary to his or her risk tolerance and investment objectives. Whether a broker may be held liable in "economic suicide" cases, may depend upon the nature and extent of the broker's involvement in the trades at issue.

Floating-Rate CMO

A CMO tranche that pays an adjustable rate of interest, tied to a representative interest rate index, such as the London Interbank Offered Rate (LIBOR), the Constant Maturity Treasury (CMT), or the Cost of Funds Index (COFI).

Front Running

An illegal activity in which a broker, brokerage firm or investment advisor takes a position in a security in advance of an action, that they know their brokerage firm (or advisory company) or a client will take, that will cause the security's price to move in a predictable fashion.

[245]

Growth

An increase in the value of an investment over time. Unlike investments that produce income, those that are designed for growth don't necessarily provide a regular source of cash.

Index Fund

A mutual fund (passively managed) which mirrors a stock, bond or other index. These funds have lower than average costs and smaller expense ratios.

Initial Public Offering (IPO)

A company's first offering of equity to public investors. The IPO must be registered.

Interest-Only Security (IO)

A security that pays only interest and not principal.

Inverse Floater

A CMO tranche that pays an adjustable rate of interest that moves in the opposite direction from movements in a representative interest rate index such as the London Interbank Offered Rate (LIBOR), the Constant Maturity Treasury (CMT) or the Cost of Funds Index (COFI).

LIBOR (London Interbank Offered Rate)

The rate banks charge each other for short-term loans.

Load

A one-time fee (commission or sales charge) charged to investors when they purchase mutual fund shares. A front-end load is paid up front and comes out of the initial investment; a back-end load is paid when money is taken out of the fund.

Markup

The amount a brokerage firm charges above the market price for securities in which it makes a market.

Modern Portfolio Theory (MPT)

The underlying theory, from which portfolio management concepts are derived, that investors seek to maximize investment returns while simultaneously minimizing investment risk. This theory is generally attributed to the economist, Harry M. Markowitz.

Mortgage Pass-Through Security

A debt instrument representing a direct interest in a pool of mortgage loans. The pass-through issuer, or servicer, collects payments on the loans in the pool and "passes through" the principal and interest to the security holders on a pro rata basis. Mortgage pass-through securities are also known as mortgage-backed securities (MBS) and participation certificates (PC).

Negative Convexity

A characteristic of CMOs, and other callable or pre-payable securities, that causes investors to have their principal returned sooner than expected in a declining interest rate environment, and later than expected in a rising interest rate environment.

Net Asset Value (NAV)

Total assets of a company/fund less all liabilities and prior charges. Net asset value per share is calculated by dividing this figure by the number of ordinary shares/units in issue.

Offer

The price at which a seller agrees to sell a security.

Par

The principal amount of a bond due at maturity.

Penny Stock

This is a stock that trades for under $1 per share. Penny stocks are highly risky. The Securities and Exchange Commission (SEC) has special regulations regarding to whom the penny stocks may be sold.

Price Earnings Ratio

Often referred to as a P/E ratio or PER; a measure of the level of confidence investors have in a company. The P/E ratio is calculated by dividing the current share price by the last published earnings per share (net profit divided by the number of ordinary shares). Generally, the higher the figure is, the higher the confidence.

Principal-Only Security (PO)

A security that pays investors principal only and not interest.

Private Placement

The sale of a bond, or other security, directly to a limited number of investors.

Pump-and-Dump

This is a classic stock fraud in which a firm, or group of firms, manipulates the market and price of a thinly traded stock by selling to a small, closed circle of public investors (pumping the stock). These holders sell out their positions in the security at the top of the market (dumping the stock), causing the price to begin to collapse, which usually sends the stock into a free fall.

Ratings

Designations used by credit rating agencies to give relative indications as to opinions of credit quality.

Real Estate Mortgage Investment Conduit (REMIC)

A pass-through investment vehicle which issues multi-class mortgage-backed securities that have certain tax and accounting advantages for issuers and investors.

Residual

A tranche which collects cash flow from collateral that remains after obligations to all the other tranches have been met.

Risk Premium

The excess investment return available from a risk-free security, usually considered to be the rate paid on short-term U.S. Treasury bills.

R-Squared

A measure of how closely the return characteristics of a security or portfolio match those of a particular market index. Typically, the S&P 500 is used as the benchmark. An R-squared value of 100 means the security has a perfect correlation with the benchmark index. In order to properly understand the meaning of an investment beta, you need to know how closely it correlates to its comparative index by measuring its R-squared.

S & P 500

Standard and Poor's company's index of 500 of the largest American corporations, as measured by market capitalization (stock price * number of shares outstanding = market capitalization).

Self-Regulating Organizations (SROs)

Organizations that regulate their members' actions outside the legal system. An SRO can establish policies and procedures that sanction members, or adjudicate disputes, without using the courts. The National Securities and Commodities Exchanges (NSCE) and FINRA are both SROs.

Selling Away

Occurs when a broker sells securities, or other investments, outside the scope of their work for the brokerage firm they work for. This is a violation of FINRA Rule 3040.

Sharpe Ratio

A measure of an investment's risk-adjusted return, using the investment's return minus the risk-free return as the numerator and the investment's standard deviation as the denominator.

Short Sale

Selling a security that the seller does not own but is committed to repurchasing eventually.

Solicited/Unsolicited Order

A solicited order is a securities transaction that results from a broker's recommendations, either directly or indirectly. An unsolicited order is one that results from an investor's request.

Spread

The difference between the bid and ask price on a security being offered for sale in the marketplace. The bid-ask spread provides an automatic profit for the firm making a market in the security, which compensates for the market maker being required to maintain an orderly market by buying from any seller or selling to any buyer.

Standard Deviation

A statistical calculation that measures the "dispersion" of all individual data points in a set, around and away, from the mean (average). In the world of investments, standard deviation is a proxy for the "volatility" of a security. A security's expected return over a given time period (e.g., annually) falls within one standard deviation above or below the mean approximately two-thirds of the time, and within two standard deviations approximately 95 percent of the time.

Stop-Loss Order

An order placed to sell a security at a particular price. If the order is placed at a price below which you bought the security, you automatically stop the loss on the investment at a particular place. If the order is placed above the price at which you bought the security but below the price at the time the order is placed, you automatically lock in a profit.

Style Drift

Measures the tendency of a fund to deviate from its specified investment style over time.

Tranche
A class of bonds in a CMO, or other type of structured finance, offering. "Tranche" is the French word for "slice."

Unauthorized Trading
Occurs when a broker buys, or sells, securities without the investor's consent.

Underwriter
A party that guarantees the proceeds to the firm from a security sale, thereby in effect taking ownership of the securities. Stated differently, a firm, usually an investment bank, that buys an issue of securities from a company and resells it to investors.

Value Fund
A mutual fund which buys primarily undervalued (as perceived by the manager) stocks with the expectation that the stocks will increase in value.

Volatility
The speed and magnitude of price changes of a security measured over a period of time. A price that often moves significantly will be considered to have a high degree of volatility.

Zero-Coupon Bond
A bond sold at a steep discount from its face value, which pays no interest.

Relevant Citations by Type of Claim

A. Breach of Contract

When a brokerage firm's contract with its customer provides that the firm will comply with regulatory requirements, the firm's violation of a [FINRA] rule is a breach of contract. "[P]laintiffs have a breach of contract claim entirely independent from any possible claim existing under Rule 405 or Article III." *Komanoff v. Mabon, Nugent & Co.,* 884 F. Supp. 848, 859-60 (2nd Circuit, S.D.N.Y. 1995).

B. Breach of Fiduciary Duty

1. Brokers owe a fiduciary duty to investors, even in non-discretionary accounts. *Ward v. Atlantic Sec. Bank*, 777 So. 2d 1144 (Fla. 3rd DCA 2001).
2. A broker or financial advisor is in a fiduciary relationship with his clients, *Byrley v. Nationwide Life Ins. Co.,* 94 Ohio App.3d 1, 18.
3. Agents employed to make, manage, or advise on investments have fiduciary obligation. *Restatement (2d) of Agency* § 425.
4. The relationship between a stockbroker and customer is that of principal and agent and is fiduciary in nature. *Conway v. Icahn & Co.,* 16 F.3d 504 (2nd Cir. 1994).
5. "[A]s a fiduciary, a broker is charged with making recommendations in the best interests of his customer even when such recommendations contradict the customer's wishes. *In re John M. Reynolds*, [1991-1992 Transfer Binder] Fed. Sec. L. Rep. (CCH) P 84,901, at page 82,314 (December 4, 1991).

C. Churning

1. A finding of churning, by the very nature of the offense, can only be based on a hindsight analysis of the entire history of a broker's management of the account and of his pattern of trading in the portfolio, in comparison to the needs and desires of the investor. Otherwise, by the time an abused client caught on to the wrongdoing, most of the damage may well have been done and the broker would be able to retain ill-gotten gain. In this respect, the situation is analogous to the more usual securities fraud cases. *Nesbit v. McNeil*, 896 F2d 380 (9th circuit, 1990). *Shad v. Dean Witter Reynolds, Inc.,* 799 F2d 530. As we noted in *Volk v. D.A. Davidson & Co.,* 816 F.2d at 1412.

[252]

2. The number of times the account needs to be turned over before the trading in the account is considered excessive has been discussed by many commentators and courts. Many follow the "2-4-6" rule "whereby the presence of [annual turnover ratio] greater than two indicates the possibility of churning, the presence of [an annual turnover ratio] greater than four establishes a presumption of churning, and an annual turnover ratio in excess of six conclusively establishes churning." *In re Magnan*, SEC Administrative Proceeding File No. 3-8370, 1995 SEC Lexis 1732 (S.E.0 July 5, 1999).

Cost to Equity Ratio

3. Besides the turnover in the account, courts have looked at the cost to equity ratio. This ratio indicates the portion of the account that is paid in commissions. A federal court determined that a cost to equity ratio of 14.8% required that the account "had to earn 14.8% annually on its investments simply to pay the commissions generated by Hutton." *Dasler v. E.F. Hutton & Co.,* 695 F.Supp 625, 630-632 (D. Minn. 1988).

Holding Periods

4. The length of time the account held securities may also indicate churning. The shorter the holding period, the more likely there is churning if the investment goals are not compatible with short holding periods. "The term in and out trading denotes the sale of all or part of a customer's portfolio, with the money reinvested in other securities, followed by the sale of the newly acquired securities. It is a practice extremely difficult for the broker to justify." *Craighead v. E.F. Hutton*, 899 F2d 485, 490 n.2 (6th Cir. 1990) (quoting *Costello v. Oppenheimer & Co.,* 711 F.2d 1361, 1369 n.9 (7th Cir. 1983)).

Broker's Control of Account

5. "Control may be established where a customer, although not granting his broker a formal power of attorney, so relies upon the broker that the latter is in a position to control the volume and frequency of transactions in the account... In addition to the control issue, it is noteworthy that the S.E.C. found churning in this matter where the investor's goal was income and growth and the turnover ratio was 4.81." *In re Reynolds,* 50 S.E.C. 805, 807 (1991 S.E.C.)

D. Damages

Attorney's Fees

1. It is well recognized, in the Second Circuit (New York state's federal circuit) and elsewhere, that an arbitrator has the "authority to grant legal fees." *See, e.g., Synergy Gas Co. v. Sasso,* 853 F.2d 59 (2d Cir.). *cert. denied,* 488 U.S. 994 (1988).

2. "A party who submits a claim for attorney's fees to an arbitration panel cannot contend that the panel lacked the authority to award attorneys' fees." *First Interregional Equity Corp. v. Haughton,* 842 F. Supp. 105 (S.D.N.Y. 1994) and *U.S. Offshore, Ltd. v. Seabulk Offshore, Ltd.,* 753 F. Supp. 86 (S.D.N.Y. 1990). See also *Stits v. Equitable Life Assur. Coc. Of US,* 2001 WL 274313 (S.D.N.Y. 2001).

3. Rule 10215 of the FINRA Code of Arbitration Procedure states: "The arbitrator shall have the authority to provide for reasonable attorneys' fee reimbursement, in whole or in part, as part of the remedy in accordance with applicable law." *Synergy Gas Co. v. Sasso,* 853 F.2d 59 (2d Cir.). *cert. denied,* 488 U.S. 994 (1988).

Well Managed Account

4. The Well Managed Account theory is an appropriate measure of damages in unsuitability cases and in churning cases. *E.g., Dasler v. E.F. Hutton,* 694 F.Supp. 624 (6th Cir. 1998).

5. The court in *Medical Associates* stated: "The proper method of calculating damages is to take the initial value of plaintiff's portfolio, adjust it by a percentage change in an appropriate index, during the relevant period, and subtract the value of the portfolio at the end of the period." Likewise, the *Hatrock* court stated: "the investor may recover (1) excessive commissions charged by the broker, and (2) the decline in value of the investor's portfolio resulting from the broker's fraudulent transactions. The recoverable decline in portfolio value is the difference between what [the claimant] would have had if the account ha[d] been handled legitimately and what he in fact had at the time the violation ended" (quotations and citations omitted) *Medical Associates v. Advest, Inc.,* 1989 Lexis 11253 (W.D.N.Y. 1989); *Hatrock v. Edward D. Jones & Co.,* 750 F.2d 767, 773-74 (9th Cir. 1984); and *In re. Drexel Burnham Lambert Group, Inc.,* 161 B.R. 902 (S.D.N.Y. 1993).

6. The New York Appellate Division confirmed that "[i]n order to approximate the trading losses caused by the broker's misconduct, it is necessary to estimate how the investor's portfolio would have fared in the absence of such misconduct" *Scalp v. Advest, Inc.*, 2003 N.Y. App. Div. LEXIS 10031

7. When a broker mishandles an account, customers may recover the difference between what [he] would have had if the account had been handled legitimately and what [he] in fact had at the time the wrongdoing ended. *Hatrock v. Edward D. Jones, Inc.*, 75 F.2d 767, 775 (9th Cir. 1984), *aff'd*, 472 U.S. 192 (1986).

Netting

8. "[Plaintiff] is correct when he states that there is no support to be found under federal or state law for the 'netting' theory [defendant] argued for here" *Kane v. Shearson Lehman Hutton, Inc.*, 916 F.2d 643, 646 (11th Cir. 1990).

Punitive Damages

9. Punitive damages are a proper remedy in a breach of fiduciary duty case. *Asa-Brand Inc. v. ADM Investor Services, Inc.*, No. 02-2373 (8th Cir. 2003).

10. Violation of firm's own internal office guidelines was factor in awarding punitive damages. *Alrich v. Thomson McKinnon Securities, Inc.*, 589 F. Supp. 683, 685 (S.D.N.Y. 1984).

11. "In a securities case, all that is needed for an award of punitive damages is the level of conduct required for an award of compensatory damages." *Comment, Punitive Damages and the Federal Securities Act. Recovery Via Pendent Jurisdiction*, 47 U. of Miss.L.Rev. 743, 761-2 (1976).

E. Failure to Diversify

1. It is widely known that 90% of any portfolio's performance depends solely upon the allocation between classes of investments (fixed vs. equities), and that most of the rest depends upon proper diversification within each asset class. See e.g., Brinson, Singer and Beebower, *Determinants of Portfolio Performance II: An Update, Financial Analysts Journal* (May/June 1991).

2. There is general agreement that it takes at least 10, and usually 15-20, non-correlated securities to achieve adequate diversification and thereby reduce nonsystematic risk. *See*

Edward Elton & Martin Gruber, Modern Portfolio Theory and Investment Analysis 31 (Wiley, 3rd ed., 1987).

3. "Under the duty of diversification, the trustee should not normally invest all or an unduly large portion of plan funds in a single security, or in any one type of security, or even in various types of securities that depend on the success of one enterprise." *Bruner v. Boatmen's Trust Co.,* 918 F.Supp. 1347, 1353 (E.D.Mo.1996). See *Marshall v. Glass/Metal Ass'n and Glaziers and Glassworkers Pension Plan,* 507 F.Supp. 378, 383-84 (D.Haw.1980) (enjoining investment of 23% of plan assets in speculative real estate project).

4. "Concentration of between 25% and 89% of the assets in one type of investment violated diversification requirement." *Whitfield v. Tomasso,* 682 F.Supp. 1287, 1301 (E.D.N.Y. 1988).

5. Putting 90% of portfolio in only 3 stocks would permit finding of lack of diversification, absent showing of special circumstances. *Jones v. O'Higgins,* 1989 U.S. Dist. LEXIS 10537 (N.D.N.Y. 1989).

F. Failure to Supervise

1. The duty to supervise is a critical component of the securities regulatory scheme and affirmative responsibilities are placed on those who have a duty to supervise. *In the matter of Quest Capital Strategies, Inc.,* 1999 WL 202487 (SEC Release No. ID-141).

2. In *Quest Capital Strategies, Inc.,* the court described appropriate supervision in the following manner:

> Supervisors have an obligation to respond vigorously and with the utmost vigilance to indications of irregularity, a supervisor cannot ignore or disregard red flags and must act decisively to detect and prevent improper activity. Indications of wrongdoing demand inquiry as well as adequate follow up and review. *Quest Capital Strategies, Inc.* at *19.

3. FINRA NTM 98-96 provides that:

> [I]t is a violation if the member and/or individual fails to enforce a supervisory system and/or written supervisory procedures.

G. Fraud / Misrepresentations / Omissions

1. Broker dealers and their registered reps are not allowed to seek exemption from liability for their own false assertions. *Blankenheim v. E.F. Hutton*, 217 Cal.App.3d 1463; *Saenz v. Whitewater Viyages, Inc.*, 226 Cal.App.3d 758.

2. One who fails to disclose material information prior to the consummation of the transaction commits fraud when he is under a duty to do so. **And the duty arises . . . because of a fiduciary or other similar relation of trust and confidence between [the parties]** [emphasis added]. *State v. Warner*, 55 Ohio St.3d 31 (1990), 52-54. [quoting the U.S. Supreme Court in *Chiarella v. United States*, 455 U.S. 222 (1980)].

3. "Although the Supreme Court gave no guidance on what constitutes a scheme, certainly a scheme can be inferred by a pattern of deception. A scheme of fraud can constitute a false representation." *Russ v. TRW, Inc.*, 59 Ohio St. 3d 42, 49 (1991).

H. Negligence

1. Negligent conduct will provide the basis for a claim for breach of fiduciary duty because a broker, as an agent, owes his customer a duty to exercise due care in executing all instructions given to him by his customer. *Rude v. Larson*, 209 N.W. 2d 709 (Minn. 1973).

I. Recommendation to Hold

1. "For purposes of these standards, the term 'recommendation' includes any advice, suggestion or other statement, written or oral, that is intended, or can reasonably be expected, to influence a customer to purchase, sell or hold a security." NYSE Interpretive Memo 90-5.

2. The court found liability for misrepresentation based on inducing the plaintiff to continue to hold stock. *AUSA Life Ins. Co. v. Ernst & Young*, 206 F.3d 200, 202 (2d Cir.2000)

3. The industry standard for measuring this fiduciary duty is made explicit in the Content Outline for the general securities registered representative exam (Test Series 7). The outline describes seven critical functions which are to be performed by registered representatives.

> (7)Monitors the customer's portfolio and makes recommendations consistent with changes in economic and financial

conditions as well as the customer's needs
and objectives.

(7-1)Routinely reviews the customer's
account to insure that investments continue
to be suitable.

(7-2)Suggest to the customer which
securities to acquire, liquidate, hold or
hedge.

(7-3)Explains how news about all issuers
financial outlook may affect the
performance of the issuer's securities.

(7-4)Determines which sources would best
answer a customer's question concerning
investments and uses information from
appropriate sources to provide the
customer with relevant information.

(7-5)Keeps customer informed about the
customer's investments.

J. Suitability (See Also Breach of Fiduciary Duty)

1. The Know Your Customer and Suitability rules of the Exchange
    and the NASD long have been regarded as the standard to
    which all brokers are held, the violation of which is tantamount
    to fraud. *Mihara v. Dean Witter & Co.,* 619 F.2d 814, 824 (9th
    Cir. 1980); *Keenan v. D.H. Blair & Co., Inc.,* 838 F. Supp. 82,
    86-87 (S.D.N.Y. 1993).

2. Broker has duty to advise the customer of all material facts
    with respect to any securities transaction he recommends,
    including the risks. But simply advising customer of the risks is
    not *sufficient* to meet the suitability rule. ("Although it is
    important for a broker to educate clients about the risks
    associated with a particular recommendation, the suitability
    rule requires more from a broker than mere risk disclosure.") *In
    re James B. Chase,* NASD Complaint No. C8A990081 (NAC
    August 15, 2001).

3. FINRA Rule 2090 (Know Your Customer) and Rule 2111
    (Suitability) require that a registered representative, when
    recommending investments, determine that such investments
    are suitable for the customer . . . A broker must make a
    customer-specific determination of suitability, and he or she
    must recommend only those securities that fit the customer's
    financial profile and investment objective. The broker must

[258]

make recommendations based on the information he or she has about the customer, rather than on speculation.

4. The omission to inform the investor that the recommended stocks were unsuitable amounts to fraud by omission and fraud by conduct. *Clark v. John Lamula Investors, Inc.*, 583 F.2d 594, 599-600 (2d Cir.1978).

5. "[A] recommendation can be unsuitable under the reasonable basis standard regardless of whether the transaction ultimately results in a profit or a loss." *Clinton H. Holland Jr.*, 52 S.E.C. 562, 566 (1995) affd, 105 F.3d 665 (9th Cir. 1997).

6. Broker has duty to advise customer of risks of a transaction. When the recommendation is a complicated one, such as a recommendation to borrow on margin, that duty requires that the broker provide the customer with detailed information sufficient to ensure that the customer truly understands what he or she is undertaking. *Vucinich v. Paine, Webber, Jackson & Curtis, Inc.*, 803 F.2d 454 (9ᵗʰ Circuit, 1984).

7. "A customer's wealth does not give a salesperson a license to disregard the customer's investment objectives." *Henry James Faragalli, Jr.*, Release No. 34-37991, 63 S.E.C. Docket 651, 1996 WL 683707 (Nov 26, 1996).

8. Even where the customer appeared to have authorized aggressive management of his account, "he could not authorize [the registered representative] to make unsuitable recommendations." Id. at p. 18. *NASD Office of Hearing Officers Department of Enforcement v. Robert Joseph Kernweis, et al.*, Disc. Proc. #CO2980024 (Feb. 16, 2000)(citations and quotations omitted).

Online Investor Resources

1. **American Association of Individual Investors:** Specializes in providing education in the area of stock investing, mutual funds, portfolio management and retirement planning.
   http://www.aaii.com/

2. **BetterInvesting:** A non-profit organization providing investment information, education, and support that empowers members to become successful, lifetime investors.
   http://blog.betterinvesting.org/

3. **Bloomberg:** Site for business and financial market news. It delivers world economic news, stock futures, stock quotes, & personal finance advice.
   http://www.bloomberg.com/

4. **BrokerCheck:** FINRA's Broker background check:
   http://www.finra.org/Investors/ToolsCalculators/BrokerCheck/index.htm

5. **Business Dictionary.com**
   http://www.businessdictionary.com/

6. **Consumer Financial Protection Bureau:** The federal agency that holds primary responsibility for regulating consumer protection in the United States.
   http://www.consumerfinance.gov/

7. **Council of Institutional Investors (CII):** A nonprofit, nonpartisan association of pension funds and other employee benefit funds and foundations. In addition, it is a leading voice for good corporate governance and strong shareowner rights. The Council's mission is to educate its members, policymakers and the public about corporate governance, shareowner rights and related investment issues, and to advocate on members' behalf.
   http://www.cii.org/about

8. **Edgar Database:** Securities and Exchange Commission's large searchable database of corporate financial reports.
   http://www.sec.gov/edgar.shtml

9. **Frequently Asked Questions:** Answers from Investopedia.
   http://www.investopedia.com/ask/answers/

10. **FINRA:** Financial Industry Regulatory Authority
    http://www.finra.org/index.htm

11. **Federal Trade Commission (FTC):** The FTC enforces a variety of federal antitrust and consumer protection laws.
    http://www.ftc.gov

12. **Fidelity:** For retirement investing, investing and/or spending, college/education investing, charitable giving.
    https://www.fidelity.com/welcome

13. **FINRA Arbitration:** An overview of the FINRA Dispute Resolution process.
    http://www.finra.org/ArbitrationAndMediation/Arbitration/Process

14. **FINRA Arbitrator Application Package:** All resources needed to become a FINRA arbitrator.
    http://www.finra.org/ArbitrationAndMediation/Arbitrators/Become anArbitrator/ApplyNow/index.htm

15. **FINRA Investor Alerts:** Read published alerts and sign up to receive new alerts from FINRA.
    http://www.finra.org/Investors/ProtectYourself/

16. **FINRA Investor Podcasts:** FINRA's Investor Podcasts discuss the timely financial issues and information you'll need to save smarter and weather today's turbulent stock markets. Investor Podcasts will also help you protect your portfolio by reporting trends in investment fraud and other traps investors at all wealth and experience levels should avoid.
    http://www.finra.org/Investors/SmartInvesting/GettingStarted/Po dcasts/

17. **Index Funds Advisors:** Index Funds Advisors provides wealth management by utilizing risk-appropriate, returns-optimized, globally diversified and tax-managed portfolios of index funds.
    http://www.ifa.com

18. **International Financial Reporting Standards (IFRSs):** Aimed at ensuring that financial statements provide information that existing and potential investors and others capital providers need to make capital allocation decisions.
http://www.ifrs.org/Investor+resources/Investors+and+IFRS.htm

19. **Investment Advisor Public Disclosure (IAPD):** Provides information about current and certain former Investment Advisor Representatives.
http://www.adviserinfo.sec.gov/IAPD/Content/Search/iapd_Search.aspx

20. **Investopedia:** Resource for investing education, personal finance, market analysis and free trading simulators.
http://www.investopedia.com

21. **Investor Bill of Rights:**
http://www.nasaa.org/Investor_Education/Investor_Bill_of_Rights

22. **Investor point:** Stock, Mutual Fund and Financial Information.
http://www.investorpoint.com/

23. **Investor Protection Trust (IPT):** The Investor Protection Trust provides independent, objective, information to help consumers make informed investment decisions. Founded in 1993 as part of a multi-state settlement to resolve charges of misconduct, IPT serves as an independent source of non-commercial investor education materials. IPT operates programs under its own auspices and uses grants to underwrite important initiatives carried out by other organizations.
http://www.investorprotection.org/

24. **InvestorsWatchdogblog.com:** An informative website that provides a daily blog with editorials, news and stories about what is happening in the securities industry. Investor's Watchdog (IW) is an investor protection company that provides investors with SEC Enforcement experience and an insider's knowledge of the securities industry to lead you around the dangers that threaten your savings.
http://www.investorswatchdog.com/investor-protection-services.htm

25. **Lawsource:** Provides access to the laws of every state.
http://www.lawsource.com/also/

26. **Michael Levy:** Author of *Cutting Truths* and *Invest With a Genius*.
http://www.pointoflife.com

27. **MyMoney.gov:** The U.S. government's website, dedicated to teaching all Americans the basics about financial education.
http://www.mymoney.gov/index.html

28. **National Bureau of Economic Research (NBER):** A private, nonprofit, nonpartisan research organization dedicated to promoting a greater understanding of how the economy works. The NBER is committed to undertaking and disseminating unbiased economic research among public policymakers, business professionals, and the academic community.
http://www.nber.org/info.html

29. **National White Collar Crime Center (NW3C):** A non-profit, membership affiliated organization comprised of law enforcement agencies, state regulatory bodies, and state and local prosecution offices. The organization provides a nationwide support for the prevention, investigation, and prosecution of economic and high-tech crimes.
www.nw3c.org

30. **NASDAQ**
http://www.nasdaq.com/

31. **North American Securities Administrators Association (NASAA):** The state and provincial securities regulators who comprise the membership of the NASAA have protected Main Street investors from fraud for 100 years, longer than any other securities regulator.
http://www.nasaa.org/

32. **New York Stock Exchange (NYSE):**
http://www.nyse.com/

33. **Office of Investor Advocacy:** The SEC's Office of Investor Education and Advocacy provides a variety of services and tools to address the problems and questions you may face as an investor.
http://www.sec.gov/investor.shtml

34. **Public Investor Arbitration Bar Association (PIABA):**
https://piaba.org/

35. **Securities Exchange Act of 1934:** Complete text.
http://taft.law.uc.edu/CCL/34Act/index.html

36. **SEC Complaint Center:**
http://www.sec.gov/complaint/select.shtml

37. **SEC Investor Alerts:** Investor Alerts and Bulletins.
http://www.sec.gov/investor/alerts.shtml

38. **SEC Law.com:** Information on State Securities Regulators. Find out who to contact in your state. In addition to the rules and regulations of the Securities and Exchange Commission, each State has its own rules and regulators.
http://www.seclaw.com/stcomm.htm

39. **SEC on Mutual Funds:**
http://www.sec.gov/investor/pubs/inwsmf.htm

40. **SEC Office of Investor Education and Advocacy:** Provides a variety of services and tools to address the problems and questions you may face as an investor.
http://www.sec.gov/investor.shtml

41. **SEC News Digest:** Index of the daily SEC News Digest, which provides daily information on recent Commission actions and business.
http://www.sec.gov/news/digest.shtml

42. **SEC Whistleblower Program:** Go to this website to report a fraud.
http://www.sec.gov/whistleblower

43. **Securities Investor Protection Corporation (SIPC):** SIPC's focus is restoring funds to investors with assets in the hands of bankrupt and otherwise financially troubled brokerage firms
http://www.sipc.org

44. **Smart Investing Forum:** A nonprofit corporation dedicated to providing generalized investment education to private and public employees, community and civic organizations, church groups, schools, and any others wishing to learn about investing. Unlike most investment education nonprofits, Smart Investing Forum is free of conflicts of interest in that it does not sell investment products and is neither directly nor indirectly supported by the securities industry or any of its members. Rather, its financial support is derived from voluntary contributions and fees for use of its services. Smart Investing Forum provides free services to qualified groups.
http://www.smartinvestingforum.org/Home_Page.html

45. **Stanford Law Securities Class Action Clearinghouse:** The Securities Class Action Clearinghouse provides detailed information relating to the prosecution, defense, and settlement of federal class action securities fraud litigation.
http://www.securities.stanford.edu/

46. **Stockpatrol.com:** Provides information which will help investors better protect themselves.
http://www.stockpatrol.com/s_investorresources.php

47. **TD Ameritrade:**
https://www.tdameritrade.com

48. **Vanguard:** Vanguard is owned by the funds themselves, with each fund contributing a set amount of capital towards shared management, marketing, and distribution services.
https://www.personal.vanguard.com/us/home

49. **Yahoo Finance:** Free stock quotes, up to date news, portfolio management resources, international market data, message boards, and mortgage rates.
http://www.finance.yahoo.com/

Further Reading

1. *13 Bankers: The Wall Street Takeover and the Next Financial Meltdown*, Simon Johnson and James Kwak, 2010.

2. *Aftershock: Protect Yourself and Profit in the Next Global Financial Meltdown*, David Wiedemer and Cindy Spitzer, 2010.

3. *All the Devils Are Here: The Hidden History of the Financial Crisis*, Bethany McLean and Joe Nocera, 2010.

4. BAILOUT, *An Inside Account of How Washington Abandoned Main Street While Rescuing Wall Street,* Neil Barofsky, 2012

5. *BAILOUT: What the Rescue of Bear Stearns and the Credit Crisis Mean For Your Investments*, John Waggoner, 2008.

6. *Barbarians of Wealth, Protecting Yourself from Today's Financial Attilas*, Sandy Franks and Sara Nunnally, 2011.

7. *The Big Investment Lie: What Your Financial Advisor Doesn't Want You to Know*, Michael Edesess, San Francisco, 2007.

8. *The Big Short, Inside the Doomsday Machine*, Michael Lewis 2010.

9. *Blood on the Street: The Sensational Inside Story of How Wall Street Analysts Duped a Generation of Investors*, Charles Gasparino, 2005.

10. *Busted: Life Inside the Great Mortgage Meltdown*, Edmund L. Andrews, 2009.

11. *The Buyout of America: How Private Equity Will Cause the Next Great Credit Crisis*, Josh Kosman, 2009.

12. *Confessions of a Subprime Lender: An Insider's Tale of Greed, Fraud, and Ignorance*, Richard Bitner, 2008.

13. *Confessions of a Wall Street Analyst: A True Story of Inside Information and Corruption in the Stock Market*, Dan Reingold with Jennifer Reingold, 2006.

14. *Cutting Truths: Fifty Enlightening Slices of Life*, Michael Levy, 2010.

15. *The Day After the Dollar Crashes: A Survival Guide for the Rise of the New World Order*, Damon Vickers, 2011.

16. *Does Your Broker Owe You Money?: If You've Lost Money in the Market and It's Your Broker's Fault--You Can Get it Back*, Dan Solin, 2004.

17. *Empire of Debt: The Rise of an Epic Financial Crisis*, William Bonner and Addison Wiggin, 2006.

18. *Endgame: The End of the Debt Supercycle and How It Changes Everything*, John Mauldin and Jonathan Tepper, 2011.

19. *Financial Shock: A 360° Look at the Subprime Mortgage Implosion, and How to Avoid the Next Financial Crisis*, Mark Zandi, 2008.

20. *Fool's Gold: How the Bold Dream of a Small Tribe at J.P. Morgan Was Corrupted by Wall Street Greed and Unleashed a Catastrophe*, Gillian Tett, 2009.

21. *Full of Bull: Do What Wall Street Does, Not What It Says, To Make Money in the Market*, Stephen T. McClellan, 2007.

22. *The Global Debt Trap: How to Escape the Danger and Build a Fortune*, Claus Vogt and Roland Leuschel, 2011.

23. *Hoodwinked: An Economic Hit Man Reveals Why the World Financial Markets Imploded--and What We Need to Do to Remake Them*, John Perkins, 2009.

24. *How to Keep From Going Broke with a Broker - A Guide to Opening, Maintaining and Surviving Your Brokerage Account*, Richard Lewins, 2010.

25. *Index Funds: The 12-Step Program for Active Investors*, Mark T Hebner, 2007.

26. *The Intelligent Investor*, Benjamin Graham, 1949.

27. *The Investment Answer: Learn to Manage Your Money & Protect Your Financial Future*, Daniel C. Goldie, CFA, CFP and Gordon S. Murray, 2011.

28. *Invest With a Genius*, Michael Levy, 2002.

29. *The Lies About Money: Achieving Financial Security and True Wealth by Avoiding the Lies Others Tell Us-- And the Lies We Tell Ourselves*, Rick Edelman, 2007.

30. *The Looting of America: How Wall Street's Game of Fantasy Finance Destroyed Our Jobs, Pensions, and Prosperity—and What We Can Do About It*, Les Leopold, 2009.

31. *Meltdown: How Greed and Corruption Shattered Our Financial System and How We Can Recover*, Katrina Vanden Heuvel and The Editors Of The Nation, 2009.

32. *Money and Power: How Goldman Sachs Came to Rule the World*, William D. Cohan, 2011.

33. *The Other Side of Wall Street: In Business It Pays to Be an Animal, In Life It Pays to Be Yourself*, Todd A. Harrison, 2011.

34. *The Pied Pipers of Wall Street: How Analysts Sell You Down the River*, Benjamin Mark Cole, 2001.

35. *The Quants: How a New Breed of Math Wizzes Conquered Wall Street and Nearly Destroyed It*, Scott Patterson, 2010.

36. *A Random Walk Down Wall Street: The Time-Tested Strategy for Successful Investing*, Burton G. Malkiel, 2011.

37. *Reckless Endangerment*, Gretchen Morgenson, 2011.

38. *Ruthless: How Enraged Investors Reclaimed Their Investments and Beat Wall Street*, Phil Trupp, 2010.

39. *The Secret Knowledge: On the Dismantling of American Culture*, David Mamet, 2011.

40. *The Smartest Investment Book You'll Ever Read: The Simple, Stress-Free Way to Reach Your Investment Goals*, Dan Solin, 2006.

41. *The Smartest 401k Book You'll Ever Read: Maximize Your Retirement Savings...the Smart Way!*, Dan Solin, 2008.

42. *The Smartest Retirement Book You'll Ever Read*, Dan Solin, 2009.

43. *Take on the Street: What Wall Street and Corporate America Don't Want You to Know and How You Can Fight Back*, Arthur Levitt, 2002.

44. *Too Big to Fail: The Inside Story of How Wall Street and Washington Fought to Save the Financial System—and Themselves*, Andrew Ross Sorkin, 2009.

45. *What Goes Up: The Uncensored History of Modern Wall Street as Told by the Bankers, Brokers, CEOs, and Scoundrels Who Made It Happen*, Eric J. Weiner 2005.

46. *Where Are the Customers' Yachts? or A Good Hard Look at Wall Street*, Fred Schwed, Jr., 1940.

47. *Who Can You Trust With Your Money? Get the Help You Need Now and Avoid Dishonest Advisors*, Bonnie Kirchner CFG, MST, 2010.